ART

CurriculumBank

KEY STAGE TWO
SCOTTISH LEVELS C-E

ART

STEPHEN BUGG

Published by Scholastic Ltd,
Villiers House,
Clarendon Avenue,
Leamington Spa,
Warwickshire CV32 5PR
Text © Stephen Bugg
© 1998 Scholastic Ltd
3 4 5 6 7 8 9 0   9 0 1 2 3 4 5 6 7

AUTHOR
STEPHEN BUGG

EDITORS
JANE BISHOP AND LIBBY RUSSELL

ASSISTANT EDITOR
LESLEY SUDLOW

SERIES DESIGNER
LYNNE JOESBURY

DESIGNER
CLARE BREWER

ILLUSTRATIONS
MAGGIE DOWNER

COVER ILLUSTRATION
JONATHAN BENTLEY

INFORMATION TECHNOLOGY CONSULTANT
MARTIN BLOWS

SCOTTISH 5–14 LINKS
MARGARET SCOTT AND SUSAN GOW

Designed using Aldus Pagemaker

British Library Cataloguing-in-Publication Data
A catalogue record for this book is available from the
British Library.

ISBN 0-590-53417-3

Contents

INTRODUCTION   5

Overview grid   11

EXPLORING AND INVESTIGATING   15

FIGURE   33

STILL LIFE   51

LANDSCAPE   67

THREE-DIMENSIONAL STUDIES   83

DESIGN   97

PHOTOCOPIABLES   111

IT links   158

Cross-curricular links   160

POSTER PACK

A poster pack to accompany this book is available from Scholastic. Comprising four full colour A2 posters, the pack provides a useful resource to enable teachers to fully exploit activities described in this book.

The four posters are:
Bizarre by Clarice Cliff;
The Playground by Laurence Stephen Lowry;
Still Life with Milk Jug and Fruit by Paul Cézanne;
Toledo by El Greco.

These have all been previously published in *Art & Craft*, Scholastic.

The Curriculum Bank Art KS2 poster pack can be purchased separately from: Scholastic Educational Books, Westfield Road, Southam, Warwickshire CV33 0JH, please quote ISBN 0 590 53754 7.

Introduction

Scholastic Curriculum Bank is a series for all primary teachers, providing an essential planning tool for devising comprehensive schemes of work as well as an easily accessible and varied bank of practical, classroom-tested activities with photocopiable resources.

Designed to help planning for and implementation of progression, differentiation and assessment, *Scholastic Curriculum Bank* offers a structured range of stimulating activities with clearly stated learning objectives that reflect the programmes of study, and detailed lesson plans that allow busy teachers to put ideas into practice with the minimum amount of preparation time. The photocopiable sheets that accompany many of the activities provide ways of integrating purposeful application of knowledge and skills, differentiation, assessment and record-keeping.

Opportunities for formative assessment are highlighted within the activities where appropriate, while separate summative assessment activities give guidelines for analysis and subsequent action. Ways of using information technology for different purposes and in different contexts, as a tool for communicating and handling information and as a means of investigating, are integrated into the activities where appropriate, and more explicit guidance is provided at the end of the book.

The series covers all the primary curriculum subjects, with separate books for Key Stages 1 and 2 or Scottish Levels A–B and C–E. It can be used as a flexible resource with any scheme, to fulfil National Curriculum and Scottish 5–14 requirements and to provide children with a variety of different learning experiences that will lead to effective acquisition of skills and knowledge.

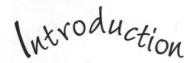

SCHOLASTIC CURRICULUM BANK ART

The *Scholastic Curriculum Bank Art* books help teachers to plan comprehensive and structured coverage of the art curriculum, and help children to develop the required skills and understanding through practical activities.

There is one book for Key Stage 1/Scottish Levels A–B and one for Key Stage 2/Scottish Levels C–E. These books reflect the programmes of study for Art in the National Curriculum for England and Wales, and in the Scottish National Guidelines.

Art is interpreted to cover art, craft and design and the ideas in this book aim to provide a comprehensive coverage of opportunities for individual and group working arrangements, a range of skills and techniques and an appreciation of work in a wide variety of genres and styles.

Lesson plans
Detailed lesson plans, under clear headings, are given for each activity. They provide ideas for a wide variety of activities covering art, craft and design. The structure for each lesson plan is as follows:

Activity title box
The information in the title box at the beginning of each activity outlines the following key aspects:
▲ *Activity title and learning objective* – Each activity has one or more clearly stated learning objectives, given in bold italics. These learning objectives break down aspects of the

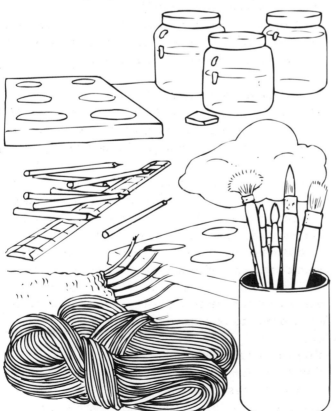

programmes of study into manageable teaching and learning units, and their purpose is to aid planning for breadth and balance. They can easily be referenced to the National Curriculum and Scottish 5–14 requirements by using the overview grids at the end of this section (pages 11 to 14).
▲ *Class organisation/likely duration* – Icons ⚥ and ⏰ signpost the suggested group sizes for each activity and the approximate amount of time required to complete it. Timing arrangements are by their nature arbitrary, as many factors are involved (including the children's previous skills and knowledge).
▲ *Safety* – Where necessary, safety considerations are flagged with the ⚠ icon.

Previous skills/knowledge needed
Information is given here when it is necessary for the children to have developed particular skills, experienced certain activities or acquired special knowledge before undertaking the activity.

Key background information
The information in this section is intended to set the scene and provide helpful guidance for you, the teacher. The guidance may relate to children's learning, to teachers' knowledge of art or to both.

Preparation
Advice is given where it is necessary either to prepare the children for the activity or to collect and prepare materials before working with the children. It is often useful to have tried out some of the activities prior to the session. This ensures that you have a knowledge of the types of activities the children will wish to try out and raises awareness of the difficulties they may encounter. Clearly this is not practical on every occasion but some activities benefit from more careful preparation.

Resources needed
All the equipment, materials and photocopiable sheets needed to carry out the activity are listed here, so that you or the children can gather them together easily before the beginning of the teaching session.

What to do
Easy-to-follow, step-by-step instructions are given for carrying out the activity, including (where appropriate) suggested points for discussion. In many cases the activity is broken down into a series of stages or sessions to achieve the overall aim.

Suggestion(s) for extension/support
Where possible, ways of providing for easy differentiation are suggested. Ways of offering support to less able pupils and ideas to extend the more able are provided. It is worth

noting that where the whole class is engaged in an activity at the same time, it is often easier to offer support, and to ensure that the children achieve the objectives set.

Assessment opportunities

Each lesson plan has clearly stated assessment opportunities which relate directly to the learning objectives for that activity and provide the framework for ongoing assessment. By taking advantage of these assessment opportunities, teachers can be reassured that the stated learning objectives have been covered.

Opportunities for IT

Where opportunities for IT present themselves, these are briefly outlined with reference to particularly suitable types of program. The 'IT links' on pages 158–159 present specific areas of IT covered in the activities, together with more detailed support on how to apply particular types of program. Selected lesson plans serve as models for other activities by providing more comprehensive guidance on the application of IT, and these are indicated by the bold page numbers on the grid and the ◈ icon at the start of an activity.

Looking at works of art

Suggestions are given for existing works of art which will enhance the children's understanding of a theme or activity. Note that 'Looking at the work of other artists', can refer equally to art students' work as to the paintings of Van Gogh or Picasso.

You will find works of art and useful resources in:
▲ poster packs accompanying these *Curriculum Bank Art* books;
▲ published art books, or posters available from other sources, including *Art & Craft* magazine (published by Scholastic);
▲ twentieth-century art books (which would be invaluable);
▲ print packs of famous art works – available at quite low cost on topics such as portraits, landscapes, buildings, animals and so on.

Display ideas

Suggestions for displaying the children's completed work are provided in this section.

Reference to photocopiable sheet(s)

Where activities include photocopiable activity sheets, notes describing how they can be used to assist you in planning are given here, together with a miniature version.

Photocopiable activity sheets

Many of the activities include photocopiable ideas which provide extensions or suggest alternative ways of working. With some, the children are required to develop imaginatively a drawing and in others to use the information provided as a stimulus for the development of a short project. In a few they are asked to add colour or texture to the actual photocopiable. While this can be an appropriate activity, the learning objective needs to be very clear. 'Colouring in' as an end in itself is very unlikely to be a valuable activity and should seldom be asked of the class or group.

Some sheets may be used for assessment purposes and would be useful as records to include in portfolios of children's work to monitor their progression in art.

Cross-curricular links

Cross-curricular links are identified on a simple grid (see page 160) which cross-references particular areas of study in art to the work which could be undertaken in other subject areas.

ART AND THE NATIONAL CURRICULUM

The visual elements

The art curriculum at Key Stage 1 is based around the children's need to develop their abilities in understanding and being able to use: line, colour, pattern, texture and form; in other words to develop their ability to use the 'visual elements'. The National Curriculum refers to these elements again in the end of Key Stage 2 statement but this time states: 'They choose materials, methods and visual elements appropriate to their intentions, making images and artefacts for different purposes'. This is a tall order for it appears to imply that the children have learned all there is to know about the visual elements by the end of Key Stage 1, and can now use them with confidence, selecting for example appropriate colours when painting, or choosing the most appropriate medium for undertaking a tonal drawing.

It is clearly important at Key Stage 2 to give the children opportunities to choose materials and processes for themselves but they also require instruction in how to use the visual elements, clear guidance and support in their use when engaged in art work and opportunities to discuss outcomes at various stages in the production of their work. The visual elements are an integral part of the language of art and underpin each activity. They need, therefore, to be to the fore of your thinking when planning, whether long, medium or short term.

Use of materials, tools and techniques

▲ Central to all art activities is drawing. The children must be given regular opportunities to draw accurately from direct observation (and at times and where appropriate from photographs, books and magazines), to draw expressing ideas and feelings, and to draw for design purposes. Sometimes the drawing may be seen as an end in itself while at others it may be investigative, as when sketching prior to engaging in other art processes. The drawing may be in pencil but it will also include charcoal, ink, crayon or paint as appropriate.

▲ A requirement of Key Stage 2 is for the children to keep a sketchbook. The physical nature of the sketchbook is not the important factor but rather the requirement is for them to record observations and ideas and to collect visual evidence and information. The first chapter of this book deals with a number of ways in which the children can further develop a wide range of important drawing skills.

▲ In addition the children should be given regular opportunities to undertake work which requires them to use colour. It is important that this includes frequent use of paint as well as crayons, coloured pencils and various types of inks and dyes. Too often children end this key stage with their minds made up that they cannot paint, equating the ability to paint with the need to be neat and tidy in their art work.

▲ Finally, the children need to be given regular opportunities to engage in three-dimensional work. A considerable minority of children find increasingly that they are able to express themselves more clearly in three dimensions rather than two. To plan art activities where there is hardly any opportunity for the child to engage in constructing, modelling or carving is to provide an inadequate art programme.

To include only these three aspects – drawing, colour and three-dimensional art – would clearly be too limited an art course. It is necessary, however, to be mindful of the time available. There is the constant danger of planning for a whole range of possible outcomes many of which will never be realised. It is better therefore to plan with a realistic set of

It is important to understand that when choosing works of art to show the children, we may either be extending or confining their knowledge. For example, if they are shown only works by the Impressionists, the Pre-Raphaelites or other essentially realistic artists, then they will have the notion reinforced that art is only concerned with representing the world as if seen through a window or by using a camera to capture the scene. These images may be easily read and shared with the class but they can also encourage the children to think that their own efforts are very much inferior. Rather than increasing their confidence it may well retard progress. It is important, therefore, to show them a wide range of art which includes examples from the twentieth century and work from other cultures.

Opportunities for looking at works of art need to be built into planning and not left to chance. It is useful to build up a range of questions to use when observing art works. These need to be based around consideration of the content of the work, speculating on the artist's intentions, evaluating the artist's use of the visual elements and comparing and contrasting with other art works. There are many questions written into activities within this book which will be of help to those teachers who require further support with this aspect of planning.

When discussing art with children it is important to remember that it is seldom a matter of right and wrong. The children (and the teacher) should feel free to speculate, discuss and evaluate what they see before them. It can be very useful to have knowledge as to the artist's intentions, but it is not vital and a great deal can be gained by both teacher and children looking at a work of art by an unknown artist for the first time. In these instances, particularly among older children, there may follow a desire to do some research.

targets and then to plan for other activities, such as printing, work with textiles and design, in conjunction with colleagues who will also be teaching the children during the key stage.

Knowledge and understanding

Learning objectives linked to developing the ability to use the visual elements, and a wide range of materials and processes when working analytically and expressively, covers the areas of investigating and making. Children are, however, also required to develop their knowledge and understanding of art. This is achieved by the children looking at and discussing works of art, craft and design. Through observing and discussing they develop a better understanding of their own work and equally importantly develop a broader understanding of the parameters of art.

This is not to suggest that it is necessary to include the study of the work of artists in each art activity the children undertake but to suggest that from time to time, where appropriate, the children are given the opportunity to look at and discuss, sometimes at length, pictures, sculptures, artefacts and prints, which are of relevance to their own artistic progress.

Most children, by the time they are eleven, wish to produce pictures in which things 'look right'. They are unlikely to understand the requirements of producing a perspective drawing but this is essentially what they wish to achieve. If they are not shown works of art by twentieth-century artists or those from other cultures then they will not be given the necessary opportunities to broaden their horizons. In understanding how a wide range of artists represent their view of the world and their feelings and ideas, the children can inform their own work, broadening and extending their repertoires.

Teaching art

Teaching art at Key Stage 2 is challenging. It requires some thought to be given to the range of experiences, skills, materials and processes which will best meet the needs of the child. It needs to be broad based and essentially practical and to build on those skills developed at Key Stage 1. The requirement to plan carefully is as important in art as it is in English, maths or science.

Children between the ages of five and seven make very rapid strides in developing important artistic skills. The vast majority of children at Key Stage 1 move through a period of representing the world through the drawing of symbols, to the beginnings of more accurate representation. In this book consideration is given to the further development of these analytical skills so that by the time the children come to the end of the key stage they are 'able to represent features of the world that they choose with increasing accuracy and attention to detail'. It is a fundamental objective that children develop the ability to record accurately where and when required.

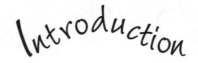

Developing the ability to record with accuracy leads to the development of confidence. As many teachers find out when attending training courses in art and design, confidence is a key factor in successfully developing artistic skills. Without some degree of confidence, progress can be severely limited and instead of ending the key stage being able to express ideas and feelings confidently, children enter the next period of their art education with an 'I can't draw' or 'I don't like painting' mentality. This may well stay with them for life.

Assessment

Assessment in art is inextricably linked to planning. If the teacher is clear as to the learning objectives then assessment can take place both during and at the end of the activity. For example, if the children are required to develop a drawing using a wide range of tones, creating an interesting range of shapes and filling their paper; then the assessment is straightforward. Have they used as wide a range of tones as possible? Do the shapes fill the paper? When assessing it is also important to ask the children to evaluate their own, and others' work. Can they see by comparing three or four of their works how some have been more successful than others? Why is it that one drawing has more interesting shapes than another? This helps them to make improvements, so developing their work.

By assessing the children's art in this way, they acquire the vocabulary of art, a better understanding of processes and the realisation of the importance of the visual elements.

Art requires, therefore, little formal assessment and recording, however, by retaining examples of the children's work through the year and where possible through the key stage, the teacher is able to track a child's progress. A good idea is to begin an assessment book with one page for each child. Do not comment after each activity but be prepared to make brief, salient comments when the child either significantly improves their understanding of an art process or produces an outcome of special significance. Over the period of the key stage this page can be added to by subsequent teachers.

Planning

The planning in this book is developed under specific chapter headings: *Exploring and investigating, Figure, Still life, Landscape, Three-dimensional studies* and *Design.* In some schools, art will be linked to topic work while in others it will be free standing. Some may decide to develop planning around consideration of the visual elements. Similarly, it is possible to incorporate a mixture of various classifications.

However the art co-ordinator and class teacher decide to categorise the planning, the key aspects to be included remain the same. They need to ensure that the children:
▲ undertake a range of processes and work in a number of materials;

▲ study and develop their understanding of the visual elements;
▲ look at and discuss the work of a wide range of artists;
▲ investigate, research, analyse, express and record the world in which they live.

When using the activities in this book you may find it helpful to be clear as to which of these objectives are relevant.

The time allocated to art at Key Stage 2 is very often less than at Key Stage 1. As the children develop literacy skills so less time is available for recording and expressing through visual means.

Careful consideration therefore needs to be given, to the range of activities to be undertaken in the hour or hour and a half which many teachers are now able to allocate to art each week. When planning, a number of decisions will need to be made concerning what is to be taught and, equally importantly, what is to be left out.

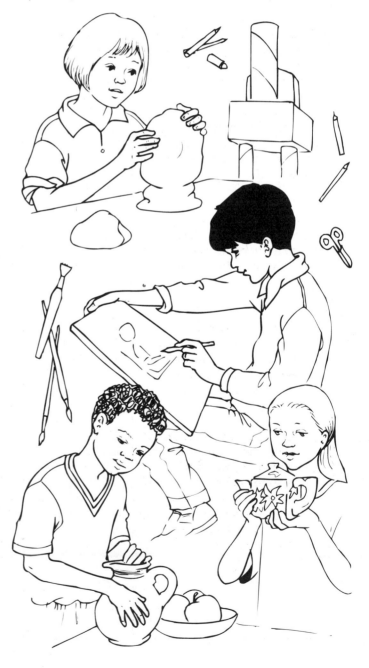

Learning objective	PoS/AO	Content	Type of activity	Page
Exploring and investigating				
To develop the ability to investigate, record observations from direct experience and collect visual evidence and information, using a sketchbook.	8a, b, c. *Investigating visually and recording, Level C*	Wide range of drawings of objects in the classroom undertaken at various times.	Whole class, groups and individuals working at various times throughout the term.	17
To observe and record accurately the process of change, ageing and decay.	1; 7a, c; 8b, e. *As above, Level D*	Sequential drawings and colour studies of fruit decaying over a period of time.	Whole class introduction, followed by small group, paired or individual art work.	20
To increase understanding of ways of creating textures through working with different types of paper.	7b; 8b, c, e. *Using media, Level C*	Experimenting with a wide range of textures working with various types of paper.	Whole class sessions supplemented by individual work undertaken at various times.	22
To look afresh at and record familiar views and objects from unusual angles. To increase awareness of shape, space and pattern.	7a; 8a, b, e. *Using visual elements, Level D*	Drawing areas of the classroom working from unusual angles.	Small groups or whole class working on individual drawings.	25
To identify the characteristics of good design. To improve understanding of the design process.	2c; 7b; 8a, b, e; 9b. *Investigating visually and recording, Level C/D*	Working from direct observation to record accurately. Follow by developing drawing into a design.	Whole class activity with pupils working in pairs.	27
To observe and record the figure in motion. To develop confidence with figure drawing.	8a, b, e. *As above*	Drawings of the figure, introducing short poses and timed drawings.	Whole class or small groups working in corner of classroom.	30
Figure				
To improve the ability to communicate feelings and ideas through art work. To develop an understanding of how artists convey messages in their paintings.	8a, c, f. *Communicating, Level C*	Personal interpretations of views and attitudes towards their own families. Art work expressing personal feeling.	Whole class or small group.	34
To communicate observations of, and feelings about, themselves. To develop analytical and compositional skills.	8b, f; 9d. *As above*	Visual descriptions of themselves, including their likes, dislikes and hobbies.	Whole class, small group or individual activity.	37
To develop drawing and painting skills through a consideration of the visual elements.	8a, e, f; 9b. *Using visual elements, Level C*	Using figure drawing as a starting point for considering the importance of line and texture.	Ideally whole class activity although also possible with small group.	38

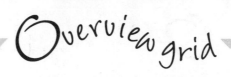
Learning objective	PoS/AO	Content	Type of activity	Page
To explore ways of improving the expression of ideas, feelings and emotions through art work.	8c, e, f; 9b, e. *Comminicating, Level C*	Exploring ways of representing emotions through developing skills in organising and using the visual elements.	Ideally whole class activity although also possible with small group.	41
To develop the skills required to work as a member of a team. To develop the ability to use an understanding of the work of a well-known artist to inform their own art work.	7e, f; 8a, c, f; 9d. *Observing, reflecting, describing and responding, Level C*	Speculating on change working from Lowry painting.	Whole class working in groups of four.	43
To develop the ability to observe and record facial characteristics using a variety of media.	7c; 8a, b, d, e, f. *Investigating visually and recording, Level C*	Portraiture, looking at proportion exaggeration as opposite ways of recording.	Whole class working in pairs drawing each other.	46
To explore the imaginative and expressive potential for art work using the human figure as the stimulus.	2a; 7a, c, d. *Creating and designing, Level C*	Illustration of a passage from a book with emphasis on the weird and wonderful.	Whole class working in groups of four. Responding to text from story.	49
Still life				
To explore shape, pattern, line and colour through looking at the work of Cézanne. To use an understanding of Cézanne's style to develop drawing and pattern skills.	7e, f; 8a, c, e. *Using visual elements, Level D*	Consideration of the importance of composition in undertaking still life work.	Whole class discussion followed by class split into groups for practical work.	52
To further develop the ability to record from direct observation. To understand the process by which drawings can be used as a stimulus for further art work. To develop a range of printmaking skills.	8a, d, e, f. *Investigating visually and recording, Level C*	Drawings of a shoe used as the stimulus for work using a wide range of process and techniques.	Whole class undertaking observational drawings. Follow up work with whole class or small groups.	55
To develop the ability to select information. To use colour and pattern to create interesting design work.	7a, b, c, d. *Using visual elements, Level C*	Selecting a section of a still life for developing colour and pattern work.	Small group activity drawing and experimenting in a corner of the classroom.	57
To use line and tone as an aid to recording directly from observation. To develop analytical skills.	8a, b, e. *Investigating and visually recording, Level D*	Intense, detailed recording of observation working from distorted image.	Suitable for whole class, small group or individuals working outside of art lesson.	60
To consider the importance of shape, space and colour when working from plants and flowers.	7e, f; 8a, b, d, f. *Using visual elements, Level C*	Working with a variety of materials and processes to record through drawing.	Whole class or small groups.	62

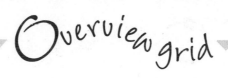

Learning objective	PoS/AO	Content	Type of activity	Page
To develop group work and the ability to use the visual elements in picture composition.	7e, f; 8a, b, e, f. *As above, Level C/D*	A series of drawings used to produce a semi abstract composition.	Groups of four pupils working as a team.	64
Landscape				
To use shapes to create rhythms and patterns. To identify the use of size and colour to signify depth. To develop clay skills including the ability to use texture.	7e, f; 8c, d, e, f. *Creating and designing, Level D*	Scrutiny of El Greco poster followed by clay interpretation. Representing 2D three-dimensionally.	Whole class introduction followed by individual work suitable for whole class or small groups.	68
To observe and record accurately from direct observation. To make adjustments in order to work as a member of a team.	8a, f. *Investigating visually and recording, Level C*	Working as part of a team to create a combined landscape from a view through a window.	Groups of six to eight working as a team.	71
To develop the ability to record landscape from various starting points. To experiment with colours and textures to create an experimental weaving.	7b, c. *Using materials techniques, skills and media, Level C/D*	Textiles project. Weaving a range of materials to create a landscape.	Whole class or small group.	73
To observe and record changing weather conditions. To create imaginative and dramatic landscapes following observations of El Greco's Toledo.	7e, f; 8a, b, d, e f. *Creating and designing, Level C*	A series of sky studies used as the source for large scale group work.	Individual recording of skies each morning followed by group work.	75
To develop the ability to take notes, sketch and collect information. To identify pattern, shape, texture and colour within a building. To work with a partner in order to achieve a shared outcome.	8b, c, d e, f. *Investigating visually and recording, Level D*	Visit to a building (church, library etc) for sketching and collection of information. Developing ideas on return to school.	Whole class visit, with children working in pairs prior to developing ideas as whole class activity.	78
To increase awareness of the rapid changes to the environment. To introduce methods for identifying distance including ways of addressing perspective.	8a, e, f. *As above, Level D/E*	Raising awareness of the local environment in particular looking at street signs and furniture. Developing design work from observations.	Whole class working from memory prior to developing individual interpretations.	80
Three-dimensional studies				
To develop understanding of three-dimensional space. To be able to work as a member of a team.	8d, e, f. *Using media, Level C*	Working with canes and tissue papers to make simple 3D shapes (sailing boats).	Group activity for 6 to 8 children working in pairs. Supervision required.	84
To develop the ability to use clay as a sculptural material. To understand how pictures often have fore/middle/backgrounds.	7e; 8c, d, e, f. *As above*	Working with clay to create a 3D landscape (with reference to a famous painting).	Activity suitable for children working in pairs. Small group or whole class.	86

Learning objective	PoS/AO	Content	Type of activity	Page
To develop the ability to display products in an interesting way.	7c, d, e, f. *Creating and designing, Level C*	Designing and making a display unit linked to Clarence Cliff poster.	Paired work for small groups or whole class.	88
To develop clay modelling skills. To produce an imaginative response to a specific brief.	8d, e, f. *As above*	Modelling figures from clay to create small group or whole class tableau.	Each pupil working on their figure independently but as member of small team or whole class.	91
To develop understanding of symbolism using colour and shape. To develop constructional skills.	8e, d, f. *As above, Level D*	Collecting information and sketching ideas prior to making a constructed monument.	Working in pairs to make a sculpture. Part of small group or whole class activity.	93
To gather resources and materials to stimulate and develop ideas.	7b, c, d. *As above, Level C*	Gathering suitable resources to make musical instruments prior to group performance.	Groups of four to eight children working as a team. Art/Music.	95
Design				
To develop the ability to communicate information using signs and symbols.	1; 2c; 8e, f. *Creating and designing Level C*	Designing and making a visual map to represent a simple journey.	Individual activity suitable for whole class.	98
To understand the importance of shape in composing designs. To develop the ability to produce abstract work through expressive design.	2c; 8a, b, c, e. *As above, Level D*	Working from observed drawings to develop designs.	Group activity for groups of approximately six children.	100
To develop understanding of the functional aspects of design.	2c; 8a, d, e. *As above*	Further observed drawings used for developing as ceramic designs.	Either whole class or group activity.	102
To design and make functional items. To work as a member of a team.	2c; 8c, d, f; 9e. *As above*	Designing and making simple jewellery and mirror frames based on sea designs.	Whole class activity with children working in groups of approximately eight.	104
To develop the use of shapes and colours to express feeling. To create a spontaneous design.	2a; 8c, e, f; 9e. *Communicating, Level D*	Responding to music using a variety of lines, colours and shapes to express feelings.	Whole class activity with children working individually.	106
To develop understanding of the roles that colour, shape and texture play in creating patterns.	2c; 8d, f. *Using visual elements, Level C*	Designing and making 'mock' board game where shape, colour and composition are emphasised.	Paired activity for whole class.	109

Exploring & investigating

One of the fundamental reasons for teaching art is to help children reach a better understanding of the world in which they live. They need time to look and to record their observations, but the world is transient and forever changing. Often it is not sufficient, therefore, for the children to do just one drawing of, for example, a flower, but rather they need to do several drawings over a number of days in order to understand some of the process of growing and decaying.

In art at Key Stage 2 children are required to use a sketchbook to record observations and ideas, and collect visual evidence and information. This exploration and investigation of the world in which they live, together with the exploration of the visual means to express their ideas and feelings, lies at the heart of good sketchbook work.

Exploration and investigation is to do with collecting information, which may be in the form of a 'complete' drawing but may be a series of unfinished drawings with notes attached, explaining how things were or appeared.

Looking at the work of other artists and examining, for example, the range of an artist's palette is also an important aspect of exploration and investigation.

SKETCHBOOKS AT KS2

One of the main changes to the art curriculum at Key Stage 2 is the need for children to record observations and ideas, and collect visual evidence and information, using a sketchbook. The term sketchbook is often misunderstood and therefore poorly interpreted. It does not necessarily mean that all children should have a sketchbook in which they undertake a drawing from time to time, but rather that they have the opportunity to experiment with techniques, make records often in 'visual' note form and collect information. It is, therefore, a way of ensuring that teachers see art as an investigative process and not simply as a picture-making activity.

A sketchbook is a collection of drawings, notes or practical experiments which are collated together to form 'a body of evidence'.

In all of the activities in this chapter the children make their own sketchbooks rather than working from manufactured ones. While you may wish the children to have their own manufactured sketchbooks which they retain throughout the school, it is often more appropriate for them to draw on to paper (approximately A4), and then to add these to 'sketchbooks' they make themselves. In this way there is not the concern about filling their books too quickly or the need to keep all their drawings clinical because they are in their 'best' books. Sketchbooks are therefore a collection of drawings and experiments which are collected together into a loose-leaf file made by the children. At its simplest the children may punch two holes in the paper and sew the sheets together adding a cover of their own design.

Where the sketchbook is made in this way there is more likelihood of the teacher allowing the children to experiment and undertake drawings individually at odd moments, when other work has been finished. One of the key reasons for having sketchbooks is that they allow the children to draw for their own enjoyment and to build up a personal selection of work, some based on the requirements of the teacher, but others completed simply because the child enjoys drawing. Children can make several sketchbooks throughout the year, each relevant to a particular topic, such as paper textures, apples and so on, and each with its own cover.

Finally, investigating and exploring may not involve drawing at all, but consist of, for example, a series of colour studies, explorations of various textures or written notes. On occasions exploration may be undertaken at the same time as a particular painting or sculpture is in progress. It is not always appropriate to see sketching as a precursor to art work, in other words designing then making. Such a process can lead to frustration, particularly where the children know what they want to do but are still required to go through some mundane, unnecessary sketching prior to beginning.

It is not, therefore, the act of having a sketchbook which is important, but rather the act of sketching, through exploration and investigation, which is fundamental to ensuring the child enjoys a rich and stimulating art education.

INVESTIGATING THE CLASSROOM

To develop the ability to investigate, record observations from direct experience and collect visual evidence and information, using a sketchbook.

†† *Whole class, small groups and individuals.*

🕐 *Approximately six 45-minute sessions per year.*

Previous skills/knowledge needed

Observational drawing should be undertaken regularly throughout children's education. This activity builds on their previous drawing experiences. Children of all abilities can follow the various aspects of this activity, producing differentiated outcomes in response to the stimulus.

Key background information

This activity lies at the heart of children's art education. Drawing from directly observed experience in order to collect visual evidence and information fully meets key requirements of the 'Investigating and Making' strand.

This activity centres on drawing objects collected by the teacher and children. The same type of activity can be undertaken starting from drawings through windows, of the

children in the class, posters of famous paintings displayed and of corners or other areas of the classroom.

Spread these observational drawing sessions throughout the year, returning at regular intervals to introduce the children to differing ways of recording information. Often the drawings can be linked to another art activity. For example, those outlined in the 'What to do' section below can be linked to many of the activities in the *Still life* chapter.

When drawing it is advantageous for the children each to have a clipboard on which to attach their paper. This allows them greater mobility within the classroom, and also to undertake some of their drawing with their paper propped up rather than on the horizontal. These separate drawings can be made into sketchbooks at the end of the sessions.

Preparation

The classroom is the most important stimulus the teacher has for introducing the children to the various requirements of observational drawing. Regardless of size, the room needs to be carefully organised. There are three ways in which a room can be organised to stimulate art work.

▲ At a minimum, two or three open shelves should be available for the collection of interesting artefacts. With the help of the children begin a collection of objects which will be of interest to investigate through drawing, such as bicycle bells, stones, bones, hub-caps, old musical instruments, roots, feathers, small pieces of machinery and bottles of different shapes and sizes.

▲ Plants help create warmth. They are also very good starting points for observational drawing. Try to have a few regularly available with interestingly shaped leaves.

▲ Finally, be prepared to make the maximum use of any views through classroom windows, whether these face inwardly on to a corridor, other classrooms, or outwards to a playground or the view beyond. At the very least, outward facing windows can be used for the children to do colour studies of, for example, variations in weather and differing cloud formations.

Make enough copies of photocopiable pages 112 and 113 for one between two, if required.

Resources needed

A collection of artefacts as outlined, A4 paper, clipboards, sketching or 2B pencils, felt-tipped pens, chalk and charcoal, wax crayons, coloured pencils, oil pastels, water-colour boxes, mirror. If required: photocopiable pages 112 and 113.

What to do

Using the artefacts collected introduce the children both to the differing ways they may record their observations and to the differing media they may use to work with. For example, in the first session ask them to work from a small object such as a shell and to magnify it several times so that the drawing fills the paper. The drawing could be undertaken using chalk and charcoal and they should concentrate on recording the various tones they observe. Follow this with a second drawing in which they use a magnifying glass to concentrate on one small section and draw in detail all they can see, this time using a pencil.

Other sessions may include the children drawing some of the following:

▲ reflections in a hub-cap, bicycle bell, Christmas bauble or kettle, using charcoal or pencil;

▲ quick, five-minute sketches of an unusually shaped stone observed from differing angles;

▲ felt-tipped pen drawings of a musical instrument in which there is no opportunity to correct their work as they progress;

▲ colour studies of a peacock's feather using oil pastels;

▲ hatched tonal drawing of an old training shoe;

▲ a section of a large piece of machinery, for example a bicycle, using a viewfinder to select a specific area;

▲ a potted plant in which they also include the area of the room in which the plant is situated (for example putting the object in context);

▲ photocopiable page 112 provides more ideas for observational drawing where the children observe themselves in different reflective objects;

▲ photocopiable page 113 provides a still life with the addition of a reflective surface – this adds another visual dimension to what the children can see.

Where it is not possible to arrange the room so that all the children can see the object, or where there are insufficient resources for the whole class to draw at the same time, then engage the class in several of the above activities at the same time, rotating as appropriate.

Suggestion(s) for extension

Encourage the children to take their drawings further either by completing drawings in their own time if they are not finished, or by undertaking other drawings of the same or a very similar object using a different media. Encourage the children to draw at home and be prepared to praise any work they wish to share, even if sometimes it does not appear to be of quite the same standard as class work.

Suggestion(s) for support

If the objective is for the children to magnify the object to fill the paper, many of the children will need support with drawing to a consistent scale in order to achieve success. For this type of activity it may be easiest to engage the whole class in the activity so that you can offer the necessary support.

You will need to make sure that they keep to the brief. Where the children undertake the activity in a small group be prepared to offer considerable support at the beginning of the activity. Once the group have satisfactorily completed the first part of their drawings they should be able to work with greater independence.

Assessment opportunities

From time to time, collect in the children's drawings and offer appropriate comments concerning the development of their sketchbooks. Look to offer praise, but also indicate areas where improvements can be made. This is equally important for those who are producing very interesting drawings as for those who are finding drawing difficult. Comments such as: 'Use a wider range of lines when you draw...' or 'Your drawings would look more interesting if you made the dark

areas much heavier...', help take the children further. Avoid making comments which refer only to the child's ability to be neat.

Opportunities for IT

The children could be given an opportunity during the year to try one of their drawings using an art package. This will give them experience of making a detailed drawing and experience the difference of doing this on the computer. They will need to be able to select different line drawing tools and appropriate colours, changing the line colour to create different tonal effects.

If the school has access to a scanner some children could scan their finished sketches to create a computer image which can be loaded into an art package. The children can then continue to work on their pictures using a different medium, altering lines, adding colour washes and more detailed colours. They may need to be shown how to enlarge the picture so that they can work in detail on part of it. They could compare this computer work with that of using traditional art materials.

Display ideas

Make sure that all children get the opportunity to display their work. In particular, look for opportunities to praise and display effort. For example, keep a small space for the 'Sketchbook of the Month', in which pages from one child's sketchbook are shown. Be prepared to show a page that has been completed outside of the lesson or at home in order to encourage others to continue drawing outside of lesson time.

Reference to photocopiable sheets

Photocopiable page 112 supports the theme of this activity and requires the children to look afresh, seeing the world in a 'different form'. They will need to concentrate fully to record what they see. Check before beginning that the reflection is sufficiently clear, otherwise the children will become frustrated and the results will be disappointing.

Page 113 develops the reflective theme above. Help the children to set up the arrangement and ensure that the mirror is secure before beginning. Check the angle from which each child is to draw to ensure they can see a sufficient area of the reflection.

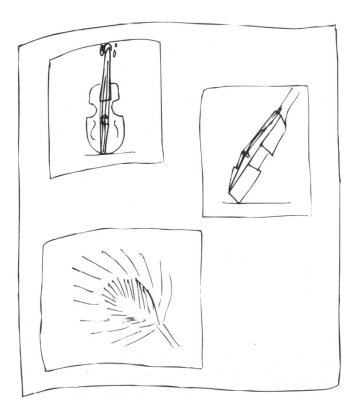

CHANGING WORLD

To observe and record accurately the process of change, ageing and decay.

✝✝ *Whole class introduction. Small groups, pairs or individual practical work.*

🕐 *Six sessions. First session 60 minutes, others 15- to 45-minutes each.*

⚠ *When studying decaying fruit, ensure it is 'under cover', for example, in a plastic bag. Do not dispose of it in school for Health and Safety reasons.*

Previous skills/knowledge needed
This activity develops practical skills learned at Key Stage 1. In particular, the children should have gained experience in mixing colours and be able to use tone and line with some confidence when drawing.

Key background information
This activity is closely linked to the children's development of scientific skills.

The children will be required to undertake a number of drawings and colour studies of one or several pieces of fruit in the process of going mouldy and decaying. The drawings will be undertaken over a period of time. The introductory session is best done with the whole class thus avoiding the need to explain the task several times to the various groups.

The activity is described using an apple as the source material. Other fruit or vegetables could be used with equal success. Alternatively, a flower or blossom may be studied as they unfurl. It may be easier to undertake the studies from a number of apples at varying stages of decay rather than observing one specimen. A further alternative is to make studies of the weather, with colour studies made over a number of days by one or more children.

Preparation
Prior to the session, experiment yourself with two or three pieces of fruit to see how long they take to decay. (Drop them on the floor two or three times to hasten the process!) Record for yourself the rate of change. This will give you a reasonable idea of the regularity with which the children should keep a record. If possible prepare the classroom for all children to paint during the first session; otherwise some will need to paint while others experiment with pastels and coloured pencils.

Arrange a small area of the classroom where the children can keep their fruit and where further drawings and paintings can be undertaken.

Ensure there are sufficient pieces of fruit for the whole class. Prepare enough copies of photocopiable page 114 for each pair of children, if required.

Resources needed
A selection of fruit, pencils (2B or sketching), coloured pencils, pastels and torn paper, water-colour boxes and pointed brushes (size 4–6), rags, scrap and white paper (approximately A4). If water-colour boxes are not available then use ready-mixed paint or powder colour. If required: photocopiable page 114, oranges brought in by the children. For extension activity: container for water, papier mâché materials.

What to do
At the beginning of the first session question the children as to assumptions we make about the nature of things. Ask them to describe an apple. Follow by asking them whether it is, for example, round, red and firm for the whole of its life. Point out that this is only one stage in the life cycle of an apple. What shape and colour is it when it first grows on the tree. How does it change shape and colour as it grows? What happens to it once it falls off the tree? How long does it take before it begins to rot? What colours occur during the period of decay and what textural changes occur? Set them a number of questions to answer over the proceeding weeks.

If you feel it is required, let the children attempt the activity on photocopiable page 114 before starting the apple task. This will prepare them for the method involved in drawing a series of pictures.

Give pairs or small groups of children one or two apples both to draw in pencil using various lines and tones, and to

colour or paint. They should produce as accurate an interpretation as possible completing both representations on one side of A4 paper. Give each child a second piece of scrap paper of a similar size on which they can experiment with colour mixing and tonal variations. Be prepared to talk to the children while they work. When using their pencils, ask them to experiment on the rough paper to see how many different tones they can make and to try drawing lines of varying strengths before beginning their studies. Encourage them to look with intensity at the apple: is the edge of the apple darker at the bottom or the top, or is there a sheen on the skin which they can reproduce?

When painting or colouring urge them to experiment with their colour mixing until they get the correct colour. Finally, suggest they add a few brief notes, for example, identifying as accurately as they can the red or green they have mixed.

This session will allow you to set the standard and give children the necessary information for undertaking further drawings and paintings of their apple as it begins to decay. Further sessions, therefore, can be undertaken by small groups of children with less teacher input. Over a period of several days or weeks the children can undertake up to six further sheets of studies through which a visual diary is established of the changes in the appearance of the apple.

At the end of the investigation ask the children to put their studies together in a simple book format. According to the time limitations, a cover of varying complexity can be designed and added. If the children are to do this, be clear as to the purpose of the activity. Having worked very hard on their studies, don't encourage the children to waste time on very low level design work which adds little to the activity.

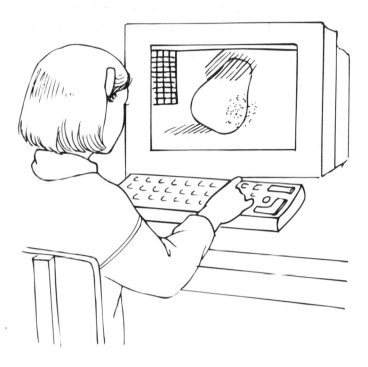

Suggestion(s) for extension

Ask the children to follow the same process but under different conditions, for example keeping the apple in water, to see whether this quickens or slows the decaying process.

Further studies could be produced three-dimensionally, making a papier mâché model of the apple at one of the stages of decay.

Suggestion(s) for support

Following the first session, when the children are given a considerable amount of support, they should be able to work largely unaided. This activity gives the children the opportunity to develop their independence. If the children are having difficulty understanding the type of drawing required, give them a copy of photocopiable page 114 to help them understand the idea of a series of pictures. Further support can be linked to assessment.

Assessment opportunities

Where an art activity is spread over a period of time, this allows the teacher to assess the child's development at various stages. Discuss with the children ways they can improve their ability to record accurately. Does each drawing and painting take less time? In cases where they are finding difficulty, make suggestions and check to see whether, in subsequent studies, they show they have benefited from the support. Note also their ability to sustain their involvement with the activity. Add to your individual notes on any child who shows particular aptitude.

Opportunities for IT

Some children could tackle this task using an art package. They should be shown how to select appropriate tools such as pencils and brushes, and how to change their size and shape to create lines of different effects. The children will also need to be able to select colours from the palette. In order to give children the chance to work in a wide range of colours you may need to select a different screen mode. They can explore the use of the spray can to help them blend different colours and create the effects seen on fruit. The children should be shown how to 'zoom' into parts of the screen so that they can work in more detail on an enlarged part of the picture.

The children will need good hand–eye co-ordination to use the mouse accurately. An alternative approach would be to use a graphics pad where children can draw with a stylus in a similar way to a pencil. The lines are then transferred to the screen.

Once the children have completed their first fruit they should save this so that they can retrieve it for the next session and work on their original picture, changing those areas which have altered over time. Each new copy should be saved, using a different name, so that at the end of the topic the children can print out all of their pictures.

The pictures could also be displayed using multi-media authoring software with a time-lapse effect, so that each picture is displayed for 10 seconds and then replaced by the next picture to give the decaying process a simple, slow-motion animation.

Looking at works of art

Show the children the work of a botanical illustrator, for example *The Country Diary of an Edwardian Lady* (by Edith Holden, Penguin). This will help them to realise how accurate observations over a period of time enable the observer to better understand the world in which they live.

Display ideas

The children's 'sketchbooks' can be displayed in a 'neat' form including only their finished studies, or they may show the complete task by adding in the sheets of experiments. If the latter is done, this will help to reinforce the process showing how the children have struggled to get the right tone or colour. This is akin to showing the workings to a difficult mathematical problem.

Reference to photocopiable sheet

Photocopiable page 114 reinforces the idea of a series of pictures but looks at dissecting an orange rather than watching an apple decay. Use the sheet as a prompt and ask the children to bring in their own piece of fruit to draw. As well as recording their observations ask the children to explore the use of a wide range of media and processes. The sheet can also be used for support, showing the idea of a series.

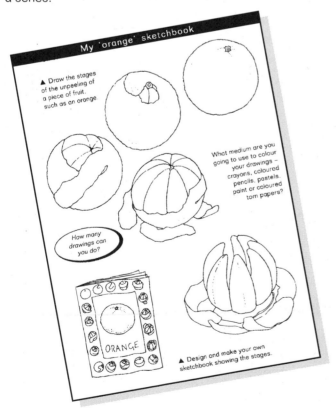

INVESTIGATING PAPER TEXTURES

To increase understanding of ways of creating textures through working with different types of paper.

†† *Whole class sessions supplemented by individual work undertaken at various times.*

⏱ *Two 45- to 60-minute sessions with other time made available.*

Previous skills/knowledge needed

While the children do not need to have previously worked on textural activities, it will be of considerable value if they have undertaken similar art work.

Key background information

This activity combines many of the requirements of the national curricula for art. The children will be required to experiment with texture, with developing control of a number of tools and techniques, and with recording their experiments using a sketchbook. Later they will be asked to reflect on and adapt their work in the light of these experiments. It is, therefore, not necessary for there always to be a finished painting or sculpture, as a series of studies can be an equally worthwhile experience for the children.

Preparation

It is worth experimenting with some ideas before beginning the activity so as to be able to guide the children in their choice of experiments.

Take one type of paper, for example brown wrapping paper, and, using both shiny and dull sides, experiment with scratching, scrunching, cutting and tearing the paper in order to discover some of the textures that can be achieved.

Resources needed
Many small pieces of white backing paper approximately 15cm × 10cm, a variety of papers (for example, wrapping, tissue, tracing, wallpaper, corrugated, blotting, newsprint and computer), scissors, adhesive, hole punch, small handsaw, erasers. For extension activity: paint, wax crayons, photocopiable page 115, glass paper, oil pastels, chalk, charcoal, brown wrapping paper, paints, brushes, kitchen roll, felt-tipped pens, coloured tissue paper.

What to do
Begin by outlining the task to the children. They should choose one type of paper and experiment to see how many ways they can find to create various textures. They might begin by scrunching up a piece of their chosen paper, then flattening and gluing it down on to the white backing paper. What type of texture do they get and how does it differ from the results obtained when using other types of paper? How else can they achieve textures using the paper alone? (They should at this stage experiment with tearing and cutting, with punching out holes using a hole punch and with roughening the surface using blunt scissors or by heavy-handed use of an eraser.) Suggest they complete five or six small experiments which can then be glued down on to the backing paper. They may find they are achieving some interesting designs as well as textures.

Ask them to use a second type of paper and to start mixing it with the first, perhaps tearing them into strips and weaving them together, as well as sticking them on top of each other or side by side. There is unlikely to be sufficient time for them to make further progress by the end of this session. Ask them, therefore, to continue this work at various times over the next two or three weeks.

This may be an activity for a wet breaktime or to be undertaken when other work has been finished. You may even suggest that they try out some experiments at home. Whichever, encourage them to pick up the activity at odd moments exploring the effects they can get by putting several different types of paper together, tearing, scrunching and cutting to create interesting textures.

Return to the whole-class activity by asking them to share their most interesting texture with each other, explaining how it was achieved. Ask them to design a cover approximately 15cm × 10cm in size for their sketchbook, on which they create an interesting pattern using various papers and leaving a space where they can add a title and their name at a later stage. Each of their experimental sheets can then be hole punched and all the pages laced together to form a small book. A plain sheet of paper can be attached to make the back cover.

Suggestion(s) for extension
Children who show an interest and rapidly create several interesting textures should be asked to widen the scope of the activity by adding colour to their samples of textures. They could also try adding wax crayon and paint (adding adhesive to the paint to make it thicker if they wish).

ART

Encourage them to experiment with colour and texture but not to worry about subject matter. In other words, if they try to paint pictures of scenes or people they will move away from the specific aim which is to look at texture.

Alternatively, photocopiable page 115 provides an activity which combines both texture and subject. The children should develop several textural collages of the apple. This would make them focus on being specific in the effect they are trying to achieve – the look of an apple – while exploring many different ways of doing it using texture.

Suggestion(s) for support

The intention is to give the children considerable initial support so that they can then develop their studies on their own. You will need, however, to check from time to time that they are able to identify a few minutes where they can continue with their experiments. Where children are unable to continue unaided, then further time will be needed during school time.

Assessment opportunities

Such investigative work allows opportunities to identify both the children's enthusiasm for the subject and their ability to work alone. Note particularly those that are able to think for themselves and come up with good ideas and those who use only the procedures outlined by yourself or other members of the class.

Looking at works of art

Many older students produce very interesting sketchbooks, often in the style the children have produced in this activity. It is worth making contact with a school or college teaching A Level or GNVQ Art, particularly if they have a textiles department, and showing the children examples of older pupils' work.

Display ideas

In order that children in other classes can appreciate the range of work produced, display your class's sketchbooks in the library rather than in the classroom.

Reference to photocopiable sheet

Photocopiable page 115 provides a learning objective which is to explore and develop the ability to use a wide range of textures focusing on an object – in this case an apple. The sheet can be used as an extension activity.

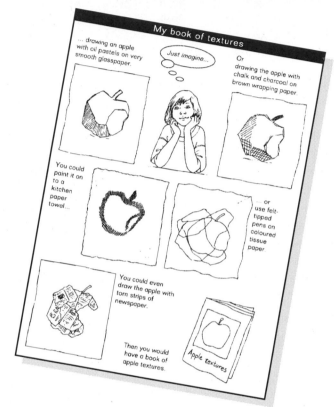

SKETCHING FROM UNUSUAL ANGLES

To look afresh at and record familiar views and objects from unusual angles. To increase awareness of shape, space and pattern.

†† *Small groups or whole class.*

🕐 *Three 60-minute sessions.*

Previous skills/knowledge needed

This activity develops issues raised in the activity 'Investigating the classroom' on page 17 where children are encouraged to look at things afresh.

Key background information

The National Curriculum requires children to select and record from first-hand information, and to reflect and adapt their work. Making choices and changes as they work should, therefore, be an integral part of their art education.

This activity questions the way in which children, and adults, observe their immediate surroundings. When we ask children to draw from observation it is almost always undertaken sitting at the desk, drawing what is directly ahead. This notion needs to be challenged. The children will be required to draw the classroom from various angles, for example sitting on the floor or from a standing position.

When teaching drawing we often emphasise the need to be accurate and neat, but fail to stress sufficiently the importance of the visual elements, for example shape, line, colour and texture. In this activity the emphasis is on shape, pattern and space. This makes the task somewhat easier. When undertaking your own thumbnail sketches (see below), and when introducing the activity to the children, firmly place the emphasis on looking for shapes creating a flat pattern on the surface of the paper. The objective is not to create a perspective drawing.

Preparation

Prior to these sessions spend a few minutes looking at the various possibilities and do two or three 'thumbnail' sketches (small drawings about 10cm square) so as to check on the likely outcomes. While there are advantages to the whole class undertaking the activity at the same time, the logistics of having all the children sitting on the floor at one time make this activity best suited to small group work. Prepare the session carefully and be clear as to the task you are setting the children.

Enlarge photocopiable page 116 to A3.

Resources needed

Paper (A4), pencils, erasers, oil pastels, wax crayons and felt-tipped pens, Cézanne, Lowry and El Greco posters (posters in the separately available pack accompanying this book), photocopiable page 116 enlarged to A3.

What to do

Begin by looking at the enlarged copy of photocopiable page 116 with the children. Having explained the idea of looking at things from different angles show the children the Cézanne poster. Ask them where they think the artist was situated when he did the painting, was he sitting or standing? What clues are there to help them decide? Show them a bowl or a jug. If they are looking at eye-level, what shape do they see? When it is placed much lower what shape do they see? Ask them to do two or three quick drawings of the bowl/ jug in different positions, looking particularly to show the shape. Look now at the other two posters showing the work of Lowry and El Greco and ask the children to decide where they think the artists had positioned themselves. If they were to draw a picture of their classroom where could they position themselves to show the room from a different viewpoint to their normal one? Given that it is difficult to be suspended from the ceiling, ask them to select an interesting viewpoint by sitting on the floor and drawing what they see under the tables. They should concentrate on the shapes and patterns they observe.

Follow by arranging a simple still-life arrangement on the floor. Ask the children to sit on chairs and draw the arrangement from above, using oil pastels or wax crayons. Again emphasise that they should concentrate on the shapes and spaces between the objects. Keep the arrangement very simple (the Cézanne arrangement is quite difficult enough for this activity).

Finally, ask the children to undertake a drawing looking through a gap in the leaves of a plant. Place a plant (a cheese plant would be ideal) very close to them so that they are

through a reflective surface (the back of a shiny spoon or a Christmas bauble – see photocopiable page 112), or through the spokes of a bicycle wheel. By leaving the project open-ended the children can produce sketchbooks of 'My pictures from unusual angles', which may include only three or many more drawings.

Discuss their drawings with them asking how they might do other ones from different angles to get more interesting outcomes. Their drawings can also be adapted to make the pattern more interesting. For example, when they have completed their drawings of under the table, look with them at the spaces and shapes in the picture and ask them to produce a simplified black and white collage. In this way they will lose any semblance of perspective and will accentuate the qualities of the pattern and shapes.

Suggestion(s) for support

Where children struggle with this task be prepared to offer them help. This may well include sitting next to a child and drawing the same view, pointing out the need to look at shape and not to be concerned with trying to draw depth. 'Just draw what you see' needs to be repeated to children time after time. Make comments like: 'Where does that line go to? What is the outline shape of that object you are drawing? Close one eye and concentrate on the outline. Keep the drawing simple, don't add too much detail'.

Assessment opportunities

Watch the children in the process of drawing identifying those who are drawing with confidence as well as those who require constant reassurance. Where you identify specific successes or difficulties add this information to the individual notes you are keeping on each child.

looking through one or two leaves at the view beyond. Ask them to choose their position carefully and to draw the shapes of the leaves and then the view beyond. By drawing with felt-tipped pens they will need to record immediately and accurately.

Suggestion(s) for extension

The three activities should be seen as a starting point for further studies and drawings. Now that the children have been encouraged to look afresh at the world around them suggest that they might do a drawing of their bedroom viewed from sitting on the floor or from the top of a flight of stairs looking down. Alternatively, they might look at the world

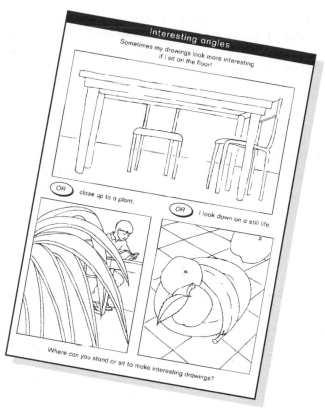

ENQUIRING INTO DESIGN: A TEA SET

To identify the characteristics of good design. To improve understanding of the design process.

†† *Whole class working in pairs.*

🕐 *Four 60-minute sessions.*

Previous skills/knowledge needed

The activity builds upon any earlier design activities the children have encountered and is most appropriate for children working towards the end of the key stage, although it could be adapted for younger children.

Key background information

It is easy to forget that art encompasses design and craft. There is a tendency, particularly when sketching, to focus on drawing from observation and to forget that such drawing can lead readily into design work. In very much the same way as children will draw designs in technology before making the item, so too in art, children should design prior to making. Sometimes the designing can be an end in itself with the actual 'making' not being necessary.

Preparation

Ensure there is a good range of flowers or foliage for all the children. To supplement the work with the poster have available several other cups and saucers which have simple floral designs and interesting shapes. Photocopiable page 144 provides background information on Clarice Cliff and her ceramic designs that you may like to have at hand throughout the activity. Page 145 provides a number of key questions to ask the children and can again be used throughout the activity. Make copies of photocopiable pages 142 to 145 as required.

Opportunities for IT

The children could use the computer to design a cover for their sketchbook. If they use an art or drawing package they can add text to their covers. Alternatively, they could use a word processor and leave a suitable space to make a sketch, or stick on one of their own drawn beforehand.

Children could also use a design package which enables them to draw an object and then view it from a variety of angles.

Looking at works of art

Reference has been made to the posters by Cézanne, Lowry and El Greco. However, almost any painting can be used to identify the position of the artist. In particular, look at the work of the Impressionists. Some of Degas' pictures of ballerinas are good for introducing this positional concept.

Display ideas

Ask the children to design a cover for their sketchbooks in which they incorporate a drawing of an everyday item from an unusual angle. Lettering for their covers can often be done on the computer, printed, cut out and pasted on. It adds to the professionalism of their work. Select two or three of the sketchbooks and place them in a prominent position in the entrance to the school for visitors to enjoy.

Reference to photocopiable sheet

Photocopiable page 116 reinforces the activity. Use it as a stimulus at the beginning of the lesson to help the children to better understand the task.

Resources needed

Poster of Clarice Cliff's ceramic work *Bizarre* (poster in separately available pack accompanying this book, or your own version), flowers and foliage, cups and saucers, paper (A4), pencils, paints, brushes, water pots, rags, a paper cup and plate for each pair of children, photocopiable pages 142 to 145, as required.

What to do

Start by discussing the poster with the children.

▲ Why do they think the designs on these pieces of crockery have become so famous?

▲ What are the common features of the work?

▲ Is colour used to emphasise shape?

▲ What differences are there in the colours on the floral designs in contrast to the landscape/abstract pieces?

▲ Does the design appear to overflow the edge of the cups or is it neatly contained within the centre?

Compare these Cliff designs with other examples you have been able to collect. Ask the children if they notice any similarities or differences. Do they know how a designer goes about producing a new set of designs?

Begin the practical activity by telling them of the work of William Morris. His biography, *William Morris by Himself* Little, Brown may provide a starting point. Morris stated that to be a good designer it is important to have an intimate knowledge of the plant, flower or bird that you are going to incorporate into your design. The task, working in pairs, is to design a floral pattern to go on to paper cups and saucers. The cups and saucers are to be used on a children's summer outing, and the design should be very bold and colourful.

From the flowers and plants that you are able to supply, ask the children to select one example and begin by making a careful and detailed observational drawing. During the follow-up session they should look to simplify their drawing concentrating on accentuating lines to make them flow. They should not be satisfied with their first drawing but go on to make several. While they work remind them that their final design needs to be in the form of a decorative band, with some element of repetition so that the design will flow around the plate or cup. Ask the children to discuss their various designs with their partner and make further alterations, if necessary, until they arrive at a successful outcome.

If possible make several photocopies of their design which they can then use to experiment with different colours. Alternatively, the children can experiment with producing patches of colour which they can place side by side to produce a simple colour chart. When painting remind them of the effects of complementary colour and of colours which they associate with warmth and summer. Remind them also of the colours in the Clarice Cliff ceramics and suggest that they try some of the colour arrangements they can observe. Suggest that within their pairs each individual tries a different range of colours. At the end they can then decide which combination they prefer.

To conclude, the pairs should either transfer the whole of their design on to a paper cup and plate or complete one section so that the effect of the design can be clearly seen.

Suggestion(s) for extension

Ask the children to design other shapes of cups and plates that would be appropriate for this summer outing. Alternatively, suggest they look at examples of crockery they have at home and make sketches of any designs that particularly appeal to them. Use photocopiable page 143 for a more structured activity to send home with the children.

Suggestion(s) for support

Be prepared to arbitrate where a consensus cannot be arrived at between the two members of the group. Use the opportunity to discuss design issues with them. For example, ask them which solution they think best fits the brief you have given them rather than which is the most attractive or colourful. Give guidance where their designs become too complicated. (The children will often attempt to produce interesting pictures rather than simple bold designs.) Remind them never to use two lines where one will do. Many professional designers struggle with what to leave out rather than what to add in.

Use photocopiable page 142 to help any children who are inhibited by the complexity of drawing a pattern for a curved shape. The sheet gives very specific points and should help the child to work through the activity in a logical progressive manner.

Assessment opportunities

Take any opportunities which arise to listen to discussion between the pairs in order to identify those children who are able to articulate and reason their decisions. At the end of the activity ask some of the pairs to present their work to the remainder of the class. Invite questions from their classmates. These may include questions such as: 'Why did you decide to use those colours?' or 'Did you consider making the shapes fill more of the cup?'

Add to your individual notes on those children where specific progress is identified.

Opportunities for IT

Some children could transfer their designs into an art package. These could be either simplified versions of their sketches or images scanned from their initial design, which could then be worked on in an art package.

The children could experiment with work in detail on an enlarged version of their design and then reduce it to create a small image for the final border.

The children could use a word processor or desktop publishing package to record the progress on their design. They could scan in their sketches and add them to the word-processed work. The images can be reduced in size and positioned on the page to create an interesting account.

Looking at works of art

Poster of Clarice Cliff's ceramic work *Bizarre* is used in this activity (separately available pack accompanying this book.)

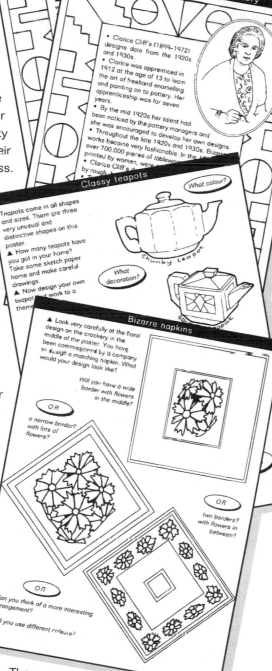

Display ideas

At the end of the activity ask the pairs to present their studies in an interesting format. If they were doing these designs for a client they would need to take their working drawings along so that they could show how they had arrived at the final conclusion. How would they present their work? They might choose to display their work in a folder, on a presentation board, on a zigzag concertina-style panel or in the form of a sketchbook. Displaying their work to maximise the quality of their designs should be seen as the final part of the activity.

Reference to photocopiable sheets

Photocopiable page 142 provides a support activity for those children who are having doubts about how to do the main task. Its structured approach should enable these children to find their confidence. Page 143 provides an extension activity that includes research at home. Page 144 is an information sheet on Clarice Cliff and her works of art. Page 145 is a set of questions that can be used throughout the activity to prompt further child response to the task in hand.

SPEEDING INTO FIGURE DRAWING

To observe and record the figure in motion. To develop confidence with figure drawing.

†† *Whole class, working in groups around tables.*

🕐 *Four 40- to 60-minute sessions , including 5- to 10-minute drawings.*

Previous skills/knowledge needed

This type of drawing is best suited to older children, who are able to demonstrate some success with analytical drawing.

Key background information

This activity further develops the children's ability to draw with confidence working from direct observation. While there are times when working from photographs is quite acceptable, where possible ask the children to draw directly from their immediate observations.

As the children progress through Key Stage 2 they often reach an age where they appear to lose confidence in their drawing. As their written work develops in sophistication so their art begins to suffer. This is particularly true of figure drawing. 'I cannot draw hands', or 'I cannot draw faces', are comments often heard. If regular opportunities are not identified for the children to undertake figure drawing then confidence often drains away. Not only do opportunities need to be written into the art curriculum but also certain skills must be taught.

There is also a temptation to slow down and take longer over drawings. While this in part is linked to the child's increased ability to sit and concentrate over longer periods of time, it can also become a way of filling in time. 'If I take long enough over this section of the drawing then I shall put off doing other areas which I think are likely to be very difficult!' seems to be the rationale that children sometimes employ. In fact, when challenged, many children enjoy being required to complete pictures very quickly. Short sharp activities often stimulate them to produce their very best work. As outlined in the next chapter, in a number of activities relating to working with the figure, teaching figure drawing needs to be carefully structured and offer a wide range of processes.

Preparation

Ensure a good environment within which the class can work. Drawing from observation requires intense concentration. Therefore settle the class before they start and get them to undertake the drawing in silence. At the end of each five- or ten-minute drawing session, allow a few moments of relaxation before evaluating and preparing for the next drawing. In this way you can constantly vary the pace and mood of the session, with short intense periods of sustained looking and recording.

A5 paper is the suggested size for the children to draw on in this activity, but you may decide that you want the children to make some of their drawings larger. Clearly this is quite acceptable, however all the activities in this section are designed to give the children confidence in undertaking

figure drawing. By working quite small they can produce little intimate drawings through which they can chart their own progress. It will also help them to see the value of keeping a small sketchbook for quick drawings and idea gathering. As they progress with their art studies this method of working will become increasingly valuable.

Prior to undertaking the task below, give the children the opportunity to do some sketches and drawings which take more than 10 minutes to complete. It does not take long to get them into the habit of recording quickly, and the practice will ensure better results when doing the 'five minute' task.

Make enough copies of photocopiable page 117 to allow one copy for each table of children.

Resources needed
White and buff paper (A5), pencils, soft black and white pastels, felt-tipped pens, erasers, photocopiable page 117.

What to do
Give each child several small pieces of paper. Hand out photocopiable page 117 to each table of children and ask them to draw, in pencil, either the classroom, or the children on their table.

Once they have completed the photocopiable sheet task, ask them to do two drawings of their hand. Allow exactly five minutes for each drawing. After the first drawing ask them to make the second more interesting by loosely clenching their hand and observing very carefully as they draw. Talk to them all the time they are drawing, 'Keep looking, draw a line and immediately have another look. How many creases are there on the finger? How many lines across the palm of the hand?' At the end of each session hold up one or two of the drawings. Again point out strengths of the drawing to the class: 'See how this drawing fills the paper.' 'Look how strong it is.' 'See how the lines vary in strength with some thick, heavy lines and others so thin you can barely see them.'

Continue by asking them to draw a portrait (head and shoulders) of the child sitting opposite them. Allow them ten minutes. Both should draw at the same time. Explain that one of the purposes of this activity is to get used to drawing a person who is not always completely still. They should look very carefully for a few seconds and then record what they have seen. Again constantly talk to them: 'See where the eyes are in relation to the ears. Can you see how heavy the line is in the middle of the mouth? Is it longer than the line of the top lip? Keep looking all the time. If you stop looking you start to make things up.' Again discuss one or two drawings at the end of the session. Ask the children what they are finding difficult, and whether they have discovered anything when doing the drawing.

Finish with another drawing, again of the same person, but this time producing a drawing of the figure down to table level.

During the first session the children can draw with pencil, making corrections as necessary; however, in the following sessions vary the media, asking them to undertake some of the drawings with a soft pastel or a felt-tipped pen. (Note: drawings of an A5 size are rather too small for using with chalk and charcoal.)

Ask for a volunteer to pose for the rest of the class. Tell the class that they are going to undertake a series of drawings of figures, posed as if in the process of undertaking day-to-day activities. For example, one pose might be bent over tying up their shoelace, another reaching up to get a book from a shelf, or in the process of putting on a jumper or combing their hair. Such poses are hard to hold even for a short time so the volunteer should rest every minute for a brief time before resuming the position. Change models for each new pose. Begin with a long pose lasting about ten minutes but then steadily reduce the time down to five minutes or less.

Make sure that all the children have a good view of the model. Arrange to do the drawings in the hall if space in the classroom is too limited. At the start of the session talk to the children: 'Can you see...? Have you noticed how...? Does your drawing fill...?' At the end of each drawing make one or two points about the drawings and ask the class to add their own comments about what they are discovering. Reassurance will also be needed: 'Don't worry if your proportions are not exactly accurate. As long as you are looking and drawing the essence of what you see, your pictures will have lots of life.' 'That's good' needs saying over and over again.

Follow this session by getting the class to draw the model (a new volunteer) posed with a prop, for example a musical instrument – they could be sitting with a 'cello, playing a recorder or strumming a guitar. If possible choose children to pose with their own instruments so that they can play while posing. Again, allow a maximum of ten minutes for drawing. The children are likely to continue to find the proportions difficult (they would be difficult for an adult!) but keep stressing the need to look and to capture the essence of the pose. By this stage if the children's confidence has been sufficiently raised they should begin to produce some very lively and vibrant drawings.

Finish by splitting a PE lesson so that while half the class carry out balance and shape activities on the floor and on apparatus, the remainder of the class can produce a number of very quick two- or three-minute drawings.

Where children begin to develop their drawing skills and show a real enthusiasm for figure drawing suggest that they do drawings in the canteen or hall, during lunch time. These might include drawings of a single person or very quick drawings of a group of people sitting round a table.

Suggestion(s) for extension

Ask for a volunteer from those who are not yet able to do extension work. Get them to do a series of poses depicting various stages of a routine activity. The more able children should do a series of drawings, one of each of the stages. For example, if the activity is bending over to tie a shoelace, the stages could be: child standing with the shoelace visibly untied; child bent half way; child tying shoelace; child standing up with shoelace visibly tied.

Suggestion(s) for support

Be prepared to offer specific support to those who find these activities very difficult. For example, it is likely that in any mixed-ability class there will be at least one or two children who find accurate recording very difficult. Look to help them make small but significant improvements and offer praise where one drawing shows a particular development.

Assessment opportunities

As this has been a significant series of drawings, collect all the children's work (stapled or sewn together to make a sketchbook) at the end of the sessions. To avoid writing on their work it is sometimes useful to make any comments you have on a Post-it note and attach it to the relevant work.

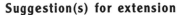

Add further comments, as appropriate, to the record you are keeping on each child.

Looking at works of art

Any book of Picasso's drawings is likely to contain examples of his figure drawing. There is probably no better artist for the children to study, to see how much can be achieved through a very economical use of line.

Display ideas

Select a few of the best or most interesting and lively drawings and take them out of the children's sketchbooks. Add quite a large 'window-framed mount' with two or three thin border lines, so as to show their drawing to the best advantage.

By adding a note to indicate how long the drawing took to complete you will be able to reinforce the notion that time is not necessarily the key issue in the achievement of high quality work.

Reference to photocopiable sheet

Photocopiable page 117 can be used as an introduction to the main activity. It gives the children the opportunity to become accustomed to working at the pace required.

Figure

The figure is a key source of inspiration for art work. Central to this work is the exploration of self, family, friends and the wider community. It is important, therefore, to ensure the children are regularly involved in art work which includes a significant figurative element. The work needs to be varied and to offer a wide range of ways of tackling the human figure. If the work constantly involves accurate representation, with proportion the most significant element, then only a small part of the figurative repertoire will have been explored. Looking at the work of a wide range of artists and exploring how they represent the human figure, will help ensure the children receive broad and relevant experience. It will also help avoid the children falling foul of the often-heard cry, 'I can't draw people!'

At Key Stage 1 the children will have been given opportunities to paint pictures of themselves and their friends and families. These will have started by being essentially symbolist, bright, colourful and often confident paintings, where all the figures have essentially similar forms. As they progressed through the key stage they will have moved towards more analytical representation, for example being able, in their drawings, to sit the figure on a chair rather than have the person standing with the chair 'stuck' to them.

Where possible figurative work should be undertaken from first-hand observation rather than working from photographs or other people's drawings.

A FRESH VIEW OF THE FAMILY

To improve the ability to communicate feelings and ideas through art work. To develop an understanding of how artists convey messages in their paintings.

†† *Whole class or small groups.*

🕐 *Up to four 60-minute sessions.*

Previous skills/knowledge needed

This is an activity that can be undertaken by children of various abilities. Where they have completed a carefully organised programme of work at Key Stage 1, they will have developed an understanding of the processes which will help them to express their feelings successfully.

Key background information

Discussing paintings or photographs allows the children to develop their understanding of the work of artists. It also gives the children's work validity and encourages them to explore for themselves a variety of ways of portraying, in this instance, the family.

Artists have produced family portraits for centuries. The infant Jesus and his family must be the most portrayed of all families, almost always shown as the perfect family with the adoring parents either holding the infant child or watching over him.

Prior to the late nineteenth century, artists produced family portraits for wealthy families for the same reason as families today have their photograph taken. Some examples of these portraits are well worth careful scrutiny by the children.

Note that this activity is giving the children the opportunity to discuss relationships through art. It is not about photographic realism.

Preparation

This activity can be undertaken quite successfully through an initial discussion with the children, followed by immediate recourse to drawing and painting. However, if you have been able to collect one or two examples of paintings in which the artist has portrayed a family, be it their own or that of someone else, then this will greatly enhance the discussion.

See 'Looking at works of art' below for suggestions as to which pictures to use with the children. If such pictures are not available then collect photographs from magazines, which also produce views of the family suggesting the varying roles and attitudes differing members of the family play.

Make copies of photocopiable page 118 for one between four or five children, if required.

Resources needed

Portraits, photographs, posters or illustrations of families, paper (A4 and A3), pencils, paints, rags, mixing trays, a variety of paintbrushes. If required: photocopiable page 118.

What to do

Show the children a number of contrasting illustrations of families. Discuss with them what the illustrations tell us about the families, perhaps picking out one or two examples for closer scrutiny. Be prepared to take some time over this, encouraging the children to look very carefully, not only at

the people in the picture but also at their surroundings. Are they portrayed indoors or outside? Are they in their own environment or elsewhere? Do they have some of their most treasured possessions (including perhaps a family pet) with them? Are they dressed in their best attire or in working clothes?

When the illustrations have been analysed ask the children to consider their own family (be sensitive to children's individual circumstances). Ask them to give some thought to whom they would like to put in their pictures. Would they include grandparents, aunts and uncles, a favourite cousin, mum and/or dad, their favourite pets, brothers and sisters? As this is to be a personal picture the children should be given considerable freedom as to the format of their family picture. If appropriate, hand out photocopiable page 118 to further the discussion.

The children should give thought to the size of the paper they use. (Bear in mind that if the work is to be a drawing on A4 paper, then the activity will be completed in two sessions, but if larger and painted, the task may take three or four.)

Having decided on the size they are going to draw, rather than go immediately into the 'final' picture, ask them to do three or four practice sketches first, working from memory. They may or may not know immediately how many members of their family they wish to include, but encourage them to try different arrangements. Are all the family members to be placed in a long line, spread around the surface of the picture or in some places touching or overlapping? (Ask the questions but do not suggest answers.) Are they to be shown indoors or outside, or is the picture to be split with some people indoors and some elsewhere? Do they wish to unite people from different places in their picture? What clothes will they wear and what possessions will surround them?

During the second session the children should finalise their family compositions and draw them on to their paper. It is worth checking each child's final composition, not necessarily to make any changes, but rather to share with them the contents of their pictures. You may also consider whether the child's final composition better suits a long thin piece of paper, rather than the traditional landscape or portrait shapes.

For the next session a decision between you and the children has to be made about

whether to paint their drawings. If the children produce extremely detailed and fine drawings you may suggest that they leave their pictures as drawings. If the children do go on to paint their pictures, suggest they leave out the smaller detail in their drawings.

So far the children will have been able to work as a whole class. However, there may not be sufficient space for all of them to paint at the same time; if this is the case, then the painting will need to be done with the children working in small groups.

Suggestion(s) for extension
This activity is an entity in itself. If, however, some of the children show a desire to take the work further, suggest that they bring into school a photograph of a member, or members, of their family from which they can then do a directly copied drawing or painting. Alternatively, they may prefer to complete a similar picture of their friends rather than their family.

Suggestion(s) for support
The support given should focus on introducing the children to the wide range of possible interpretations of the family. Once they begin to draw what may be very personal interpretations be wary about interrupting them. For example, some children may well produce hierarchical pictures with people sized according to their importance. In contrast, a few may start to overlap their figures to create a more complex interpretation. Such variations are unimportant, for, as we have highlighted in the 'Key background information', the learning objectives are to communicate feelings and ideas and to understand how others do the same.

When they are painting be prepared to give 'technical' advice as required.

Assessment opportunities
Be aware of the contributions the children make during discussions. As the children produce their initial sketches, note also their ability to make changes. Considerable variations in technical ability will also be apparent in their final drawings or paintings, even though the most interesting or moving picture may be achieved by one of the lower attaining artists. Add to your individual notes retained on each child where you feel it is pertinent.

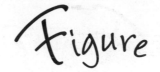
Looking at works of art

Christmas greetings cards provide an endless source of pictures of Jesus with his parents. These are generally paintings completed during the Renaissance or Victorian times. It is, however, worth looking for other examples: Henry Moore in particular produced both drawings and sculptures not only of mother and child but also of families.

Other pictures of 'the family' include *Mr and Mrs Andrews* by Gainsborough (seventeenth century) and *Mr and Mrs Clark and Percy* by Hockney (twentieth century). These contain no children but they do give a good idea of how the artist portrays a family in their surroundings. In one, husband and wife stand very closely together, in the other some distance apart. (Both pictures were used for the poster in the September 1995 edition of *Art & Craft* magazine.)

Perhaps the most interesting picture to show the children, however, is *The Bellelli Family* by Degas, used in *Art & Craft* magazine, December 1997. (A very good illustration of this painting, with useful accompanying text, can be found in *The Techniques of the Impressionists* by Anthea Callen [QED Publishing Ltd].) Here is a family that appears not to be perfect, where father sits with his back to the artist and mother stands on the other side of the room with an arm around one of her daughters. The second daughter sits commanding the centre of the picture, confident and a little apart from both parents. Here lies a wealth of detective work

for the children and the opportunity to explain their own interpretation of the picture. It also offers a valuable lead in to discussion about family life which is not the conventional one as portrayed in so many of the advertisements the children see on television.

Other examples should be considered prior to the session, for example Goya produced a painting of *The Family of King Charles IV* in which he included grandparents, aunts and uncles and some cousins. In contrast, many artists have produced portraits of mother and child or mother and children.

Display ideas

This is one instance where you may decide to display all their work in one tight-knit collection. In this way the extended families of the whole class will produce a huge frieze of people and animals packed together.

Reference to photocopiable sheet

Photocopiable page 118 can be used as a prompt to further discussion of family portraits.

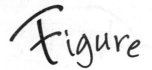

ME AND MY FAVOURITE THINGS

To communicate observations of, and feelings about, themselves. To develop analytical and compositional skills.

†† *Small group or whole class depending on available space.*

🕐 *Three 45- to 60-minute sessions.*

Previous skills/knowledge needed

This activity is similar in requirement to the previous activity 'A fresh view of the family'. Vary the content of sessions, however, by not using these activities concurrently.

Key background information

In the previous activity where the children were encouraged to produce personal interpretations, considerable freedom of compositional organisation was required. In this instance the children are required to work to a more structured format. This allows the opportunity to introduce notions of shape, space and pattern. Experimenting with the visual elements and with materials and processes while engaged on 'picture making', gives you a quite specific teaching role.

Preparation

If you decide to ask the children to work from photographs of themselves then they will need to be collected before the session. If working from mirrors make sure there are sufficient available. Make enough copies of photocopiable page 119 for one between two children.

Resources needed

Mirrors or photographs of children, white or grey paper (approximately A3), charcoal or sketching pencils, paints, mixing trays, rags, newspaper and water pots, photocopiable page 119. For extension activity: photographs of the children and their hobbies, collage materials.

What to do

Introduce the children to the notion of sending a visual message, a picture/map which must be simple to read and understand. Discuss photocopiable page 119 with them. Are these the typical possessions of a ten-year-old boy? Are they typical prized possessions of a girl also? Make sure you avoid the task turning into an advertisement for Manchester United and be wary of stereotyping!

The children will be asked to draw pictures of themselves surrounded by their personal 'treasures', or images depicting their hobbies and interests. Explain to them that their pictures need to be as clear as possible as they are to be rolled up, sealed in a container and sent on the next space probe into outer space. If the space ship is intercepted and the contents

explored then their pictures will be 'read' by someone who has no knowledge of life on this planet, and it will act as a 'map' of themselves.

Engage the class in a discussion not only of what they might include in their pictures but also how they might depict their favourite possessions, hobbies or interests. They should then spend a little while prior to starting the picture listing the possibilities and producing sketches. Before they start, share some of their ideas, highlighting some of their drawings which succinctly fulfil the requirements.

Once the discussion as to how best to depict the various elements is completed the children can start on their final work. Using photographs or mirrors to aid the self-portraits, they can then begin to add the remaining information.

Suggestion(s) for extension

With either the whole class or those children finishing early, consider asking them to follow their drawn and painted pictures by producing a collage in which they include a photograph of themselves (or a like photograph of a boy or girl if their own photographs are too valuable to destroy). They could use photographs of their interests and hobbies for part of the collage.

Suggestion(s) for support

Bring the children back together from time to time to evaluate progress and to share ideas. Comments such as: 'Look how Gary has shown a football match', or 'See how Lynne has filled the paper with only small spaces between her drawings', encourage the children to build on each other's achievements. In particular, be prepared to help them to organise the various components of the picture. They will also need reminding that they are to paint their pictures and, therefore, should not include too much information in their initial drawings. When painting remind them to keep their

designs simple and to avoid a confusing mass of detail in their compositions, so they will be easier to read by the recipients.

Assessment opportunities

At the end of the task evaluate the outcomes with the children. Ask them what they feel is successful about their picture, not only as a complete one, but also individual items within their pictures. What is it that makes one picture more successful than another? Again, add to individual notes on each child where appropriate.

Looking at works of art

While this activity can be successfully undertaken without recourse to looking at the work of other artists, you may consider it worthwhile to show the children, either at the beginning or at the end of the activity, examples of Egyptian art. In the same way as the children have prepared information for those in outer space, so the Egyptians prepared information for the Gods.

Display ideas

Wall mount some of their 'maps' and lightly roll up and tie others and display on a table. Invite children to unroll the work and to decide who is depicted in the painting. They can also decipher their interests and hobbies.

Reference to photocopiable sheet

Photocopiable page 119 is to be used at the beginning of activity to prepare the children for the main activity.

EXPLORING THE VISUAL ELEMENTS

To develop drawing and painting skills through a consideration of the visual elements.

†† *Whole class and small groups.*

🕐 *Four 60-minute sessions.*

Previous skills/knowledge needed

This activity can be undertaken at various times during the children's art education. In this instance, however, the task is aimed at raising awareness of the importance of using line, colour, shape and pattern when drawing and painting the human figure.

Key background information

Many of the requirements of the national curricula are met by this activity. Considering the work of other artists at the completion of one drawing and before another, offers a useful opportunity to evaluate the impact that looking at works of art can have on influencing and developing the children's work.

Preparation

As with many of the activities it is very useful to have looked at the work of one or two well-known artists before beginning the work with the children. Many twentieth-century artists have drawn or painted portraits of the seated figure concentrating on decoration and pattern rather than on a

Figure

off the ink bed and you should discover a textured monoprint on the backing paper. The result can be extremely pleasing and enhance the qualities of the original drawing. In particular, the prints will include an interesting textural quality where additional ink has been transferred to the paper.

When reading through the 'What to do' section below give careful consideration to the organisation of this activity. If possible arrange to undertake at least the first drawing task and, if it is to be included, the observation of the work of another artist, as a whole class. This allows you to set the scene and to make the key teaching points to the whole class. Because of space problems the remaining tasks may need to be done with the children working in small groups.

It is worth giving consideration to the conditions under which the children will work. As a rule of thumb the children will need to work in almost complete silence when observing and recording, as intense concentration is required if they are to produce quality work. When painting or printing, however, opportunities to discuss and share ideas and discoveries mean that the children will need to talk to one another.

Resources needed

A print/poster of the work of at least one artist showing a seated figure – this should display aspects of pattern and shape, and preferably decorative colour, both A3 and A4 white paper, pencils, printing inks, rollers, boards or sheets of perspex, sticky tape, charcoal, paints, appropriate brushes, rags, water pots, mixing trays, newspaper. For support activity: photocopiable page 120.

What to do

As with all activities the result will be less successful if the children rush the drawing in their enthusiasm to reach the printing stage. You may decide, therefore, not to tell them they are to do a monoprint until the drawing is completed.

Ask the class or group to draw in pencil, on A4 paper, a model who is posed sitting comfortably on a chair reading a book. Encourage them to look carefully, and to record accurately what they can see. They need not necessarily draw the whole of the model but may end their drawing at around the knees. It is important, however, for them to fill the paper with their drawing. Allow as much time as the children feel is necessary.

Children finishing quite quickly can profitably spend some time on a second drawing in which you ask them to concentrate on producing differing qualities of line. End the session by demonstrating to them how to produce a

photographic interpretation. In particular, look for examples of portraits by Matisse (for example *The Purple Robe*, or *Romanian Blouse*), although Modigliani, Jawlensky or any one of a number of twentieth-century artists will do equally as well.

Ideally, obtain a large print/poster which you can show to the whole class so that they can benefit from it by looking and discussing the artist's style. If this is not possible then a smaller print can be observed by groups of children with the whole class taking turns. By spending some time looking at the work of art before the session you will be able to acquaint yourself with the way the artist has used shapes, patterns, line and colour. The activity identifies several tasks, one of which is to produce a monoprint. If you have not done this with the children before then it is useful to try one yourself first. It will take only a few minutes.

Making a monoprint

Start by doing a quick simple drawing, the subject matter is unimportant. Roll out a small amount of water-based printing ink on to a board or piece of perspex to cover at least the same area as your drawing. The key to success is to ensure that the ink is virtually dry. If it is thick and sticky you are unlikely to achieve a successful print. Use sticky tape to attach a thin piece of white paper to the back of your drawing and lay both pieces on to the ink bed with the drawing facing up. Trace over your drawing. When finished, lift the paper

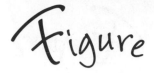

How does this artist's work compare with their own? Can they produce a drawing in much the same style? They can then try a second drawing using charcoal, and working on a larger piece of paper in which they look specifically for shapes and patterns. The background can also be patterned, and to help them consider shapes and patterns, ask the model to pose in front of a cloth or curtain which contains large bold shapes.

The drawing completed, they can then paint in bright, flat areas of colour rather than attempting to match the natural colours. (The model does not need to pose during the painting sessions.) If possible have the print/poster displayed so that the children can keep returning to it to see how the artist created a particular effect.

If the children are not to be shown the work of an artist then, before starting the second drawing, a rigorous discussion needs to be held to ensure they clearly understand the task.

Suggestion(s) for extension

Ask those children finishing early, and possibly the whole class, to do a print of their second portrait. This can be done by the children drawing a copy of their portraits on to a flat piece of polystyrene (or 'press print') and producing a one-colour print. Producing prints from their paintings will help the children to consider further shape and pattern.

Suggestion(s) for support

When the children are drawing, offer advice where required. In particular, ensure that the children work to an appropriate size. It is, for example, very difficult to produce bold, interesting drawings if their work covers only half of the paper. You may decide to offer them only minimal advice when they are completing their first drawings, but then to talk and offer a considerable amount of advice when they are involved with their second drawings. Give out photocopiable page 120 to any children who need support when monoprinting.

Assessment opportunities

As well as looking at the children's work for evidence of developing confidence in their figure drawing, look also to see how the drawings of a number of children change once they have been introduced to the work of another artist, especially after you have engaged them in considerable discussion about the requirements of the task.

Consider retaining one or two examples of the most interesting work to add to a school portfolio highlighting the standards and range of work produced by the children throughout the key stage.

Looking at works of art

Use prints/posters of portraits by Matisse (for example *The Purple Robe*, or *Romanian Blouse*), Modigliani and Jawlensky as explained above.

monoprint of their portraits. A small area can be set aside for the whole class, in turn, to produce their monoprints.

Discuss children's first drawings as a whole class, asking them to concentrate on the qualities of the shapes they produced rather than on whether they have been able to get a likeness of the model.
▲ Have they any repeating lines creating certain rhythms?
▲ Do their lines join to create interesting shapes and patterns?
▲ Is the drawing large and bold or are the shapes and patterns very small, swamped by the surrounding space of the paper?
▲ How could they improve their drawings if they were to repeat the task?

If available, introduce them to the print/poster of a portrait by Matisse, or another appropriate artist. Ask them to look very carefully, concentrating for a short time before making any comment. Steer the discussion to include consideration of how the artist has used line, shape, pattern and colour.

Display ideas

Ask the children to select the drawing, print or painting which they are most pleased with. They can then mount this for themselves either using plain backing paper or producing a patterned frame to complement their pictures.

Reference to photocopiable sheet

Photocopiable page 120 reinforces the monoprinting activity and can be used for support.

LOOKING AT EMOTIONS

To explore ways of improving the expression of ideas, feelings and emotions through art work.
†† *Small groups or whole class.*
🕐 *Four 60-minute sessions.*

Key background information

As with the activity 'A fresh view of the family' on page 34, this activity requires the children to consider an issue which is likely to concern them either at the present time or in their recent past. Some careful thought needs to be given to the introductory discussion as sensitive issues are likely to be raised. Raising issues to do with loneliness, illness, bullying or bereavement also offers opportunities to link art with work in the other arts, language and PSE.

These issues are dealt with by many artists. For example, Van Gogh and Rembrandt evoke strong feelings of the loneliness of the individual through their self-portraits. See 'Looking at works of art' below for ideas. While it is not necessary to introduce the class or group to any of these pictures when introducing the activity, consideration of one or more of them can provide a good way into the art work.

Preparation

By undertaking a few simple 'exercises' with the children before they begin their final art work you will help the children to acquire the skills and processes to express themselves.

Make enough copies of photocopiable page 121 to give one copy to each child.

Resources needed

Paper (grey, buff or a dark activity paper may be better than white), charcoal or soft sketching pencils, paints, brushes, mixing trays and rags, photocopiable page 121. If required: any relevant works of art.

For extension activity: pencils, paper, a copy of *Letters from Provence*, (Collins & Brown Limited).

What to do

The activity can be introduced in a variety of ways. It may result from work in another area of the curriculum, for example drama or language, from a theme in an assembly, or may be instigated through the art curriculum.

You may decide to begin by looking at the work of one or more artists, perhaps using the examples cited in the 'Looking at works of art' section. Alternatively, you may wish to reflect with the children on one particular issue, for example the loneliness felt after falling out with friends, the feelings engendered by a period of illness, or the loss of a favourite pet.

Hand out a copy of photocopiable page 121 to each child and ask them to complete it. This will give them an idea of what is required of them in the main activity.

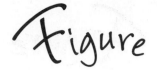

Spend some time in discussion, leading on to how an artist might try to portray the feeling of illness in a painting (or sculpture, although the children will not be attempting this). Begin by considering the colours which would best suit the mood of the picture. Is illness blue, grey, red or yellow? Would the lines used be round and smooth or long and thin? Would the paint be applied very thinly or thickly? Would paint be the best medium to use or would it be more appropriate to use pastels or collage?

The children may well disagree as to the best solution. Ask them to undertake some experiments before beginning. They should try out some colour studies on sketching paper as well as experimenting with a variety of textures before any consideration of the subject matter has taken place. Discuss the results of these studies with them.

They can now turn to a consideration of the subject matter. Again, it is good practice for them to try out two or three 'thumbnail' sketches before starting. While the way in which they portray their feelings may be very personal you may still feel the need to make suggestions. In particular, check that the final composition builds on their studies. There is often a tendency to draw the figures proportionally smaller when enlarging a study and the child may need this brought to their attention. One way to help overcome this tendency is to get the children to draw using charcoal rather than pencil.

The media used may vary depending on the choice of the children. The finished work is likely to be more interesting if some of them have used pastel or collage rather than paint.

Suggestion(s) for extension

Works of art make their own statements whether done by children or acknowledged masters. Nevertheless, our appreciation of paintings can be enhanced by either extending our knowledge about the artist or reading something the artist has written about the work. Van Gogh wrote many letters to his brother, and these provide an excellent example (see *Letters from Provence*, Collins & Brown Limited).

Ask the children to write about their pictures, perhaps starting with: 'In my picture I have tried to...'. Alternatively they might write about being ill or falling out with their friends, in an attempt to convey feelings through another form.

Suggestion(s) for support

Be careful about notions of right and wrong when asking the children to express a feeling or emotion. It may be that while we think the child should use, say yellow and green to express the feeling of illness, they wish to work in very different colours. Instead, rely on the child asking for help when they feel they are having difficulty expressing themselves.

Assessment opportunities

Look for examples of how the child is developing the ability to organise the art process. Are they able to undertake meaningful studies, to make decisions and then to develop their ideas in their final work? Add to individual notes kept on each child where significant progress is identified.

Opportunities for IT

Some children might like to use an art package to create a picture showing their emotions. They may need to be shown how to select colours from a larger palette to obtain a range of tones of a particular colour to express their emotions. They may also need to use wide brushes or spray can tools to enhance their work.

Children could also write about their pictures using a word processor. If their writing is to be displayed along with their pictures, either on the wall or in a book form, they may need to present it in a form which represents the mood of the display, changing the font style, size or colour.

Looking at works of art

Self-portraits by Van Gogh and Rembrandt, as described in 'Preparation' above, provide good examples of emotional work. Munch (a forerunner of Expressionism) portrays in his painting of *The Scream* an unknown fear. Many other Expressionist artists produced equally disturbing images. The separately available posters that accompany this book can be used to introduce the theme of unhappiness or anxiety. The Lowry poster contains several figures who may be selected and identified as looking lonely or downcast, while the El Greco poster landscape manages to create a sense of foreboding, as if some frightening event is about to occur.

Display ideas

Where the children undertake written work as well as drawing and painting, consider displaying their work in book form

anger

envy

rather than on the wall. This may be particularly apt for this activity where the work is likely to be of a very personal nature.

Reference to photocopiable sheet

Photocopiable page 121 requires class or group discussion led by you prior to the children starting the activity. It allows the children to chart the way they feel in colour, so developing their understanding of the use of colour in portraying emotions. The questions on the sheet can form the basis of the discussion but time needs to be given to talking about the issues as well as recording ideas.

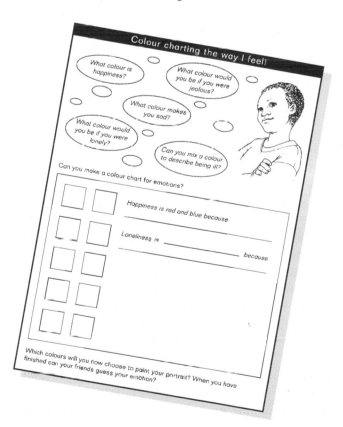

STARTING FROM LOWRY

To develop the skills required to work as a member of a team. To develop the ability to use an understanding of the work of a well-known artist to inform their own art work.

†† *Whole class working in groups of four.*

🕐 *Three or four 60-minute sessions.*

Previous skills/knowledge needed

Although older children are likely to have more success at building the various elements into a complete whole, this activity is suitable for all children at Key Stage 2.

Key background information

The national curricula require children to develop both understanding and knowledge of the work of other artists. While there are clearly benefits from children developing factual knowledge, you need to be very clear as to the importance and value of giving more than a very limited number of facts. For example, the children should know that Lowry painted a world he was born into and knew well. The vast majority of his paintings are of people going about their daily lives in and around the towns and cities of Lancashire. We generally associate his paintings with urban life in the 1930s and 1940s. The value of going beyond this, to look up passages about Lowry in books and rewriting, even if in their own words, is doubtful, unless the child shows a real enthusiasm and wishes to explore the artist's work further in their own time. Photocopiable page 148 provides more background information on Lowry.

The emphasis should be on developing the child's understanding of the painting or sculpture, and on building their ability to interpret the work for themselves. It is more important, therefore, that the child is able to discuss the way in which the artist uses colour, or the way in which the artist creates mood, than to know the date of the artist's birth or into which movement art historians have slotted him.

This has important consequences for you as it means that it is not necessary to develop a detailed knowledge before discussing the work. Instead it is far more important that you develop the confidence to explore works of art with the children and are able to use the language of art (for example: line, colour, shape, pattern and so on) to supplement discussions concerning content.

Looking at the work of artists can transform the way in which the children undertake a task. If you were to ask the children to produce scenes from the playground without first showing them the work of an artist, such as Lowry, the results would often be fairly predictable. By looking in depth at the poster, by discussing how the artist achieves mood and feeling and how he is able to tell a story, we are able to help the children develop a variety of notations with which they can achieve similar outcomes. Pictures which tell stories are

43

ART

wonderful for analysing and create a wealth of opportunities for developing skills in a variety of art forms.

In the vast majority of Western art, artists use perspective to create a sense of depth. Thus we can see the frame of the picture as a window through which we are able to view the artist's world. So, for example, when preparing to use this poster with the children you might consider suggesting to them that they imagine they are looking out of a bedroom window on the other side of the street. This would allow you to invite the children to speculate about what might happen next, to imagine what people are saying to each other, to empathise with the feelings and thoughts of one or more figures in the painting and to consider and discuss wider issues of relationships, for example loneliness or falling out with friends.

Preparation

Be prepared to spend a little while looking at the poster prior to the session so as to fully familiarise yourself with the work. If you are hesitant about discussing works of art with the children then prepare some questions beforehand.

Photocopiable page 149 provides relevant questions that can be used throughout the activity.

While art work is essentially practical and not written, there are times when it is useful to make a few notes, or even to link with English or drama, to develop the follow-up work through other art forms.

Make copies of photocopiable pages 146 to 149, as required.

Resources needed

Poster of Lowry's work entitled *The Playground* (poster in separately available pack accompanying this book, or your own version), pencils, paints, brushes, water pots, rags, mixing trays, scissors, paper, adhesive, photocopiable pages 146 to 149 as required.

What to do

Begin by introducing the children to the poster. There is a great deal to be studied within this, so ask them to look in silence for some time, studying the detail carefully before starting the discussion. Remove the poster and discuss the work from memory in order to ascertain how closely they have observed it. Use the questions from photocopiable page

149, supplementing or replacing with questions of your own, if preferred. Allow the children sufficient time not only to answer questions, but to ask more before replacing the poster and discussing it further.

You may or may not decide to undertake some written or dramatic work linked to the discussion about the poster, but develop the art work by asking the children to recreate a similar scene using the Lowry picture as a stimulus. They should, however, create a scene of life in their own school playground. Use photocopiable sheet 147 if necessary, as a prompt to help the children focus on the activity.

Organise the children into groups of four. Explain that each group is to create the view from one window pane looking out on to the school playground. The group must decide on a small tableau consisting of four people. Ask them to do quick sketches as they discuss the possibilities so that the vision is shared and not simply a scene in the imagination of one or two more vocal members of the group. They may decide they wish to portray children playing on or with some apparatus which is made available to them, or perhaps standing around talking. Disagreements are likely to occur within the groups and members may be excluded – be prepared to arbitrate in these situations.

Once the decisions have been made, each person within the group is responsible for drawing and painting one figure. Care should be taken that figures correspond in size and fit the agreed composition. There should also be some dialogue between the groups to check that all are working to a similar scale.

The groups can then work on their figures, drawing, painting and cutting them out before bringing them together to arrange them on to their 'window pane'. If there is to be apparatus, for example a swing or slide, then the group needs to add this, but at this stage do not allow them to complete the background.

Bring representatives of each group together to share progress. Once the figures are completed, they should decide in which order to arrange the 'window panes' to create the most interesting effect. They should also decide which colours to paint the background and what content to add to ensure a cohesive outcome. Some lines may need to be added to each section to ensure that they link together

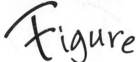

successfully. Each group can then complete their section.

When finished, the groups should assemble their work on a wall where all the 'window panes' can be displayed together.

Suggestion(s) for extension

Greater realism can be given to the project by asking the children to add the window frame, sill and curtains. A vase of flowers might also be drawn and painted and added to the final display.

Extend the children's understanding of colour producing mood in a painting by asking them to do the activity on photocopiable page 146.

Suggestion(s) for support

During the practical sessions be prepared to arbitrate where the group find difficulty in achieving a consensus. Make sure also, especially at the sketching and drawing stage, that the groups are working to a similar scale (there is likely to be at least one group whose figures are far too small!). When the groups come together with their 'window panes' towards the end of the project be prepared to offer ideas and support where necessary, although, ideally, it will be better if the children solve the problems for themselves.

Assessment opportunities

Move around the groups noting where consensus is arrived at through discussion or where one person tries to dominate the discussion. As with other activities make individual notes where children make a significant contribution or produce a drawing and painting which shows clear signs of development.

Looking at works of art

Besides Lowry it is well worth looking for a copy of *Children's Games* by Bruegel, which will give a good insight into the same type of subject matter, painted by an artist working several centuries before Lowry (see photocopiable page 147).

Display ideas

Display the final work as a whole-class tableau of children playing in the school playground, developed from their observations of the work of Lowry. The work will look more impressive if the frame to the window and other accessories have been added.

Reference to photocopiable sheets

Photocopiable page 146 can be used as an extension sheet to further the children's understanding of the use of colour. Page 147 can be used to focus the children on some key points they should be considering in the main activity. Page 148 is an information sheet on Lowry. Page 149 provides a set of questions that can be used to prompt the children as they go through the main activity.

Figure

MY FRIEND'S FACE

To develop the ability to observe and record facial characteristics using a variety of media.

†† *Whole class in pairs.*

🕐 *Four or five sessions of approximately 60 minutes.*

⚠ *Make sure the children are closely supervised when using the lino-cutting tools.*

Previous skills/knowledge needed

Lino printing, in particular, is an activity best suited to older Key Stage 2 children.

Key background information

As children develop confidence with their drawing so they become increasingly frustrated when they 'don't do it right'. For example, their attempts to represent noses and mouths may well be failures as far as they are concerned and eyes will look dull and lifeless. At this stage they will ask questions and require answers. This activity offers them the opportunity to see that there is more than one way of achieving accuracy. In the first part of the activity they are asked to draw the portrait of the person sitting opposite them, concentrating on capturing the character of the person. They should then produce studies using a variety of media, and conclude by looking at proportion and various notations with which they can produce more accurate representations.

Preparation

Little preparation is required. Ensure the room is arranged so that the children can observe each other closely and draw as they look.

There is no reason why older children should not lino print, but this does need careful supervision, and each child should have a sawing block to rest their lino against – it will help ensure that they are not tempted to place their supporting hand on the wrong side of the lino. (See illustration above.)

Most lino supplied these days is sufficiently pliable for the children to be able to cut into it with ease. If, however, they have difficulty, then warm the lino by either putting it on a radiator for a few minutes or running hot water over it.

Make enough copies of photocopiable page 122 for each pair of children to have one.

Resources needed

White or buff drawing paper, A4 or A3 in size depending on space available, coloured pastels or chalks (fixative if using chalks), lino or stiff card and other textured papers, adhesive, scissors and lino-cutting tools, sawing blocks, rollers and printing inks, clay, wire loop, 2B or sketching pencils, photocopiable page 122. For extension activity: a mirror.

What to do

Chalks or pastels

Sit the children opposite each other so that they can observe and draw almost simultaneously. (It need not necessarily be a friend, indeed it may be better if it is not!) Supply them with drawing paper and chalks or pastels. During the first session they will draw a portrait of each other. Hand out photocopiable page 122 to each pair. Explain that it provides two ideas on how to go about their drawing. Be prepared to watch closely to see they follow the processes as described.

Talk to them as they work. For example: 'Start with the eyes. Begin in the middle of the paper and work outwards – do not start with an outline of the head and then infill. Look carefully, what colour do you see, particularly around the eyes? Can you exaggerate the colour and the shapes to give the drawing more life? Are there freckles, a dimple on the chin or a rosy colour to the cheeks? Is the hair straight or curly, is it behind the ears or covering them?'

By continually asking questions while the children are drawing you are ensuring that they constantly look in order to solve problems. At this stage do not suggest solutions, for example by pointing out to them that the eyes come half way down the head or in line with the ears. This may or may not be so, but the purpose of this part of the activity is for the children to look for detail and expression rather than for proportional accuracy. By exaggerations of detail and colour, or the distance between parts of the face, the children will come to produce lively vibrant drawings. At the end of the session discuss some of the outcomes with them. Ask questions in an attempt to discover why some drawings have greater vitality than others.

Working from their first drawing the children can continue to produce two further studies using different media. Consider offering them a choice, perhaps selecting two from three different media: collage, clay or printing.

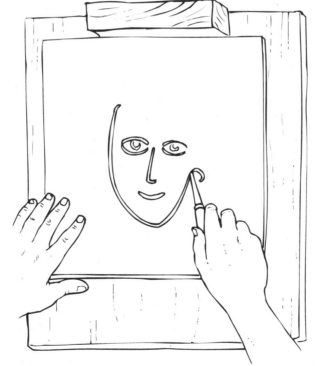

ART

Collage

The children could make a collage using a range of differing types of paper, emphasising tone or colour depending on the type of papers you make available. (Note: collages are generally most successful when all the papers are stuck down flat rather than scrunched in an attempt to make the hair or nose stand out.) Similarly exciting results can be obtained by asking the children to tear rather than cut the shapes they wish to include. In all their work, whether collage or pastel, the best results will often be achieved by building up layers rather than relying on the first colour or piece of paper to complete the task.

Printing

The children can print in one of two ways. Either they can start with a piece of thick card and build up the surface by sticking on various textured papers, pieces of string and other textured materials, or they can make cuts in a piece of lino (or smooth polystyrene). Some schools may still have simple hand-turned printing presses available but failing this, to print, lay the paper on top of the card or lino, press down firmly but carefully, and 'burnish' the back using a large spoon. By printing at various times in the process and not waiting until all the cutting or adding has been completed, a print of two or three colours can be produced.

Clay

The children may begin either with a ball of clay, into which they dig out and add on features, or with a slab of clay which they lay over a ball of paper to create the face. If the children create a whole solid head then do not fire this without extracting some of the interior with a wire loop tool first. Very thick clay has a definite tendency to blow up during firing!

Completing the activity

Throughout each of the above three tasks the emphasis has been on expression and exploring the potential of the media. Now ask the children to undertake a drawing, concentrating on accuracy of proportion. Tell them to start with the eyes and work outwards. Ask questions to ensure they continue to look very carefully:

▲ How big is the distance between the eyes?
▲ How long is the nose in comparison to one eye? (One eye, one and a half, two?)
▲ What is the distance between the nose and the centre line of the mouth?
▲ Which of the three lines that make up the mouth is the longest – the middle, top or bottom? Which is the darkest?
▲ Where do the ears come in relation to the eyes, and where do the eyes come in relation to the whole head?
▲ When shading (or completing the line drawing), can you see the reflection of what looks like a window, in the person's eyes you are observing? Does it make your drawing more interesting if you add this feature?

Using this method you will avoid giving the children stereotypical solutions but will encourage them to look at each of these features every time they produce a portrait.

Suggestion(s) for extension

The work can be followed up or added to in many ways, either at the time, for example giving those children finishing first another task, or by involving the whole class in extension work at a later date as an opportunity to put previous learning into practice. Suggest that they try a self-portrait working from a mirror, exploring the dimensions and characteristics of their own face. Where possible require them to work from 'real' people rather than from photographs, which are a very poor second best.

Suggestion(s) for support

The support in this activity has been identified through whole-class questioning. Individual children may, however, require support if they have difficulty measuring the length of the nose or capturing the precise feel and colour of the skin. Be prepared to give the children this help, either by working directly on the child's drawing if both you and the child feel comfortable with this, or by explaining through drawing on scrap paper and then allowing the child to make the necessary correction to her or his own work.

Assessment opportunities

The objectives change during this activity, from looking at capturing character and expression to experimenting with various media and finally to looking at accurate proportion and representation. In any assessment that you undertake be careful to assess using the appropriate objectives as your key indicator. For example, do not point out inconsistencies in the proportions of the face in a drawing where the children were exploring lino as a medium and trying to express the characteristics of the sitter.

Looking at works of art

The most common subject matter in art is the human face and there is a huge choice of portraits which can be used to show the children. The most widely used examples are the portraits and self-portraits produced by Van Gogh. Be prepared, however, to be more adventurous, and look for examples of portraits by Picasso, Klee, Matisse or Giacometti. Discuss with the children in some detail how these artists have portrayed the human face and ask them what type of character they think the artist was trying to depict.

Display ideas

Display their portraits mixing the chalk/pastel drawings, prints, clay and pencil sketches together. When displaying a range of work of various sizes, it is a good idea to work to a straight horizontal top line to which all the pictures can be aligned. Later fill in the space under the smaller works with another small drawing or print. It is not important that the bottom line is also straight.

Reference to photocopiable sheet

Photocopiable page 122 suggests two ways of beginning a portrait other than drawing the outline of the head. The objective is to get the children to think about the process of drawing as well as the content.

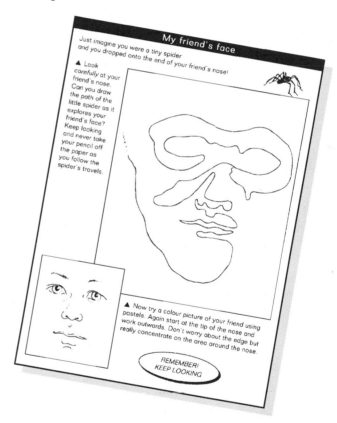

THE WEIRD AND WONDERFUL

To explore the imaginative and expressive potential for art work using the human figure as the stimulus.

†† *Whole class working in groups of four.*

⏲ *Four 60-minute sessions.*

Previous skills/knowledge needed

The work the children may have undertaken on line, tone, colour, pattern and texture will give them the means by which they can now express imaginative ideas.

Key background information

It is important to give the children opportunities from time to time to work together as a group. This will encourage them not only to consider subject matter, for example who is to do which figure, but also to consider how the shapes are going to fit into the final composition, and which colours and textures are to be used to link the figures together. By working in groups not only will they use the visual elements but they will also need to discuss them and come to shared and agreed decisions. The children in their groups (preferably of four, although you may decide on slightly smaller or larger sizes) will each produce an individual figure which will then fit into an overall composition agreed by the group.

This activity requires the children to work from descriptions of people. The descriptions should be vivid, allowing the opportunity for the children to express some highly imaginative interpretations.

Preparation

Consideration needs to be given to the available space and a decision made as to whether all the groups can work at the same time. Consider also the size of the figures and the final mural. While there are great benefits to the children working to a large scale, equally impressive results can be obtained with the children producing individual figures no larger than A4. Decide (or through previous discussion let the children decide) on a textual stimulus prior to the first session. Use something which takes them away from the normal. An excellent example would be an extract from *The Witches* by Roald Dahl (Red Fox).

Make sure that whatever the description you use, the vision is of something 'weird and wonderful' which will allow the children to give full rein to their imaginations. This is their opportunity to be surrealist in their outcomes.

Resources needed

Paper for figures and for background mural, paints, brushes (ensure a good selection of both pointed and rounded brushes), rags, water pots, mixing trays, scissors, adhesive, pencils, weird and wonderful extract as stimulus. For extension activity: balloons, wooden sticks, plaster of Paris or Mod Roc.

What to do

Organise the class into appropriately-sized groups. Introduce them to the passage you wish them to describe, or through previous discussions with the class ask them to identify the passages they intend to use.

The groups should now decide:

▲ Who is to portray which character.

▲ What pose each figure is to take in order to create an interesting composition.

▲ Any colour theme, pattern or texture to be used to link the figures.

Encourage the children to rough out a number of ideas before beginning, discussing among themselves which composition is the most dramatic and how their own figure is to fit into the overall arrangement. They should also undertake some colour and texture experiments and agree on the method and style by which they will work. Make sure that they do this carefully, not letting them start until they

have solved key questions. They need to be aware that they are not creating four totally independent figures which they then try to put together but rather that all their figures should harmonise, almost as if done by the same person. At this stage remind them of the importance of having interesting negative spaces as well as exciting positive shapes:

▲ Does the space around some of the figures flow with, perhaps, the figures touching each other or the edge of the paper while there are quite large spaces in other areas?

▲ Do the figures create a rhythm with, perhaps, the shape of one being mirrored by another?

▲ Are the figures in dramatic pose, with arms outstretched or legs and bodies contorted into grotesque positions?

When agreement has been reached they can begin work on their individual figures. Once drawn and cut out they can check the final composition before painting. If one figure is

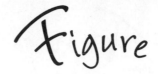

too small or fails to fit into the agreed composition then redrawing may be required. The figures can then be painted or decorated, the children sharing the colours they have mixed and differing textures they have collected.

They should then lay their figures on to the backing paper and decide on a background. If the figures produce interesting shapes and patterns, then the background need only be simple. Ask the children, for example, to try tearing strips of paper and laying these under their figures in order to assess whether this alone will help exaggerate the shapes and movement in the figures.

Suggestion(s) for extension

This theme is easily expressed through three-dimensional work. Rather than the children working individually ask them to work in pairs to create a papier mâché head of one of the weird and wonderful figures. They can begin with a balloon as a base for the head, adding detail once they have built up the papier mâché. Bodies can be added by working on top of a very simple wooden armature made from tying sticks together. Although messy and needing careful organisation exciting effects can be produced by dipping cloth into plaster of Paris, wrapping it around the stick armature and allowing to dry. Mod Roc is a plaster impregnated bandage which could be used as a further alternative. It is more expensive but rather less messy.

Suggestion(s) for support

When working in groups, particularly on a surrealist theme, there is a tendency for the children to want to rush into the work without giving due regard to the art process. Make sure, therefore, that they try out a number of ideas before they begin and that there is some genuine dialogue within the groups. While the children should make changes as they proceed, nevertheless, the key decisions need to be made before they begin. It is worth asking them discuss their ideas with you before they begin the final work.

Assessment opportunities

Group work offers the opportunity for you to visit each of the groups and to ask the children to explain how they have arrived at a particular decision. Why, for example, have they decided to place the figures in a particular arrangement? What other ways did they consider? Who made the final decision? How are they making sure it looks like all the figures were done by the same person? In this way it is possible to have a dialogue with the children about the process as well as to

assess the final outcome. Where relevant add to your individual notes on each child indicating their ability, or otherwise, to work within a group.

Opportunities for IT

The children could use a word processor to present the extract that was used as a stimulus for the work. This could be presented in suitable fonts, colours and sizes to represent the theme of the picture.

Children could also scan some of the sketches they may have made and add these to the word-processed text to make it look more interesting.

Looking at works of art

While there may be illustrations that accompany the chosen extract ask the children to ignore them. As good as some of the illustrations may be (for example Quentin Blake's illustrations are quite superb in *The Witches*), the aim of the project is for the children to use their own imaginations and not to rely on that of a professional illustrator. At the end of the project you may decide to look at the illustrator's work but only to provide a comparison to show how the group might have proceeded!

Display ideas

Try placing all the murals together to create one long frieze of the weird and wonderful.

Alternatively, consider adding a border around each individual mural on which the children write out the passage which inspired the work. If the writing goes all the way round the border facing inwards so that it is upside-down along the bottom and 'sideways' along the two edges, this can add interest to the overall work. It will also encourage other children to try to read it and then to consider whether the group have achieved their intention.

Still life

Allowing children not only to observe, but also to handle, discuss and record their observations of diverse objects such as roots, bones and old musical instruments, can act as a great stimulus to art work. It is important, therefore, to build up a wide range of items which can be used as a stimulus for art lessons and to display them, either in the classroom, or elsewhere in the school. The objects may be drawn singularly or as part of a group, perhaps undertaken in a range of media and materials.

Remember that 'difficult' objects often make good works of art. Have high expectations of the children and be prepared to set them challenging activities. For example, a composition which includes fruit, a large-leafed plant, a table and a musical instrument will often look visually interesting in a drawing which is technically quite simple.

Where an arrangement is to be the focus of the art work, think about the composition. Don't sit the children so close that they cannot properly observe the relationships between the objects, nor to pack the objects too close together that the individual shapes cannot be observed.

Looking is hard work and the children should be encouraged to undertake it with full concentration. There are times for sharing information and ideas but there are others when silence is required.

Finally be clear as to the learning objectives. Why are the children undertaking the drawing? For example, is it to be accurate in their recording? or, to explore the differing qualities of line they can use?

FRUIT, JUGS AND CÉZANNE

To explore shape, pattern, line and colour through looking at the work of Cézanne. To use an understanding of Cézanne's style to develop drawing and painting skills.

†† *Whole class in groups.*

🕒 *Two or three 60-minute sessions.*

Previous skills/knowledge needed

This activity is suitable for children at any point in the key stage. It does, however, encompass some important teaching points and is therefore placed at the beginning of this section. Children who have followed a structured programme at Key Stage 1 will readily understand the reference to the visual elements of art. Other children, however, will need to be given more time to come to terms with the issues raised.

Key background information

Children working at Key Stage 2 need opportunities to develop further their understanding and use of the visual elements. By looking at the work of other artists and analysing the way in which they use the visual elements the children will begin to understand the processes involved in art activities.

Spend a few minutes before the first session looking at the Cézanne poster very carefully (from the separately available poster pack that accompanies this book). Look particularly at his use of the visual elements: shape, pattern, texture, line and colour.

Begin by considering the composition, looking at the way in which Cézanne arranges the objects. Note the shapes and pattern. Some of the fruit overlap, others are isolated. Trace the space with your finger, working your way from the left-hand side of the table until you come to the edge on the right. By doing this you will quickly come to the realisation that the space is constantly changing, sometimes with large areas of table, sometimes with very small.

If you imagine the fruit as silhouettes then the shape of the table itself becomes interesting. We may call this shape the *negative space*. It is important that the children realise that this negative space must be interesting if their pictures are to 'work'. (How often do the children draw very small items in the middle of their paper thus surrounding the objects with overpowering or uninteresting space, or bunch all the objects so closely together that they become like a solid mass?) When helping the children to set up their own still life use this understanding of Cézanne's composition to arrange the objects in an interesting and varied way.

Now consider Cézanne's use of colour, in particular noting how he uses complementary colours. When selecting fruit, cloths or backing paper try to introduce this notion of

complementary colours, bringing it to the attention of the children.

Complementary colours

Complementary colours are colours which are opposite each other on the colour wheel. Thus red is opposite to green and blue to orange. These pairs of colours are known as complementary because by placing a green apple next to a red one or against a red table cloth the full intensity of the green will be realised.

The manner in which Cézanne applies the colour is also interesting, for while we might encourage the children to put on a thin colour wash to start with so as to cover the background, Cézanne shows us almost every brushstroke. (He often worked in oils which are perfect for this effect, although the same can be obtained from water-colours.) Dabbed patches of colour help give the painting a vitality, and make the table look almost as if it is rippling across the surface 'gripping hold' of the fruit.

Finally, note Cézanne's use of line. In some areas there appears to be a very strong, dark line and in others the line almost disappears. Look particularly at the fruit on the plate. Where is the line at its darkest? Does it correspond to areas where there are shadows?

In both the way in which Cézanne applies paint and uses line, there are important lessons to be learned as to how we might ask the children to undertake their pictures looking at line and texture. Are they able to vary the strength of the line when drawing or to apply colour in patches?

Still life

Preparation

Having studied the Cézanne poster as described in 'Key background information' above, you can prepare the still life for the children. When arranging for the children to create their own still-life compositions, give some thought to the organisation of the room. Too often children are to be found drawing and painting in the most crowded of conditions sitting on top of the arrangement with no opportunity to observe it from a distance.

You may decide that it is best to start the activity with all the children looking at, and discussing the poster together, and then split the class into groups working in turns in an area of the classroom arranged for the purpose.

Make sure that the children do not work with objects on the same eye-level. Either have the children stand and look down on the arrangement, or place it on a board propped at the back by two bricks, thereby sloping it forward so that the children are 'looking into' the jug or bowl. Make copies of photocopiable pages 150 to 153, as required.

Resources needed

Poster of Cézanne's work *Still Life with Milk Jug and Fruit*, still-life objects, enough for one still life per group (fruit, bowl or plate, jug and cloth or backing paper), blue, grey or buff paper (A3 or A4), sketching pencils, paints, firm brushes, mixing trays, rags and water pots, oil pastels, printing inks, card, photocopiable pages 150 to 153 as required.

What to do

Start by showing the whole class the poster. Discuss with the children the various elements as outlined in the 'Key background information' section. Encourage them to look very carefully, to be analytical, and to be very precise in their use of language to describe the various elements. Allow as much time as necessary.

Photocopiable page 153 provides more questions that will help the children to analyse the work. Use this as you feel necessary.

Working in groups, all at the same time if space permits, in rotation otherwise, ask one member of each group to set up a still life from the objects supplied. All members of the group should then undertake a quick, small sketch. They can then take turns at arranging a composition, and at the end, the various compositions can be discussed and compared.

Through looking carefully at the poster and analysing it in this way both you and the children will come to a better understanding of the physical process of 'making' a picture. You will also be ready to answer awkward questions like: 'Why isn't the back of the table straight?' or, 'Why do the fruit look like they are about to fall off the edge of the table?' To this you will be able to reply that the artist was trying to balance his picture, he was trying to make the shapes interesting and lively, and was concerned with thinking very hard about how a picture is built up combining all the various elements.

Photocopiable page 152 provides more background on Cézanne and his work.

Give out photocopiable page 151 and ask the children to complete it. This will put them in the right frame of mind for the next part of the activity. Now, choosing the most appropriate composition, the children can undertake a careful, detailed drawing. Ask them to add colour, applying the paint with stiff brushes in dabs and patches of colour rather than by colour washing. You may also suggest that the children start with the objects and add the background later, working in the opposite way to what they are used to.

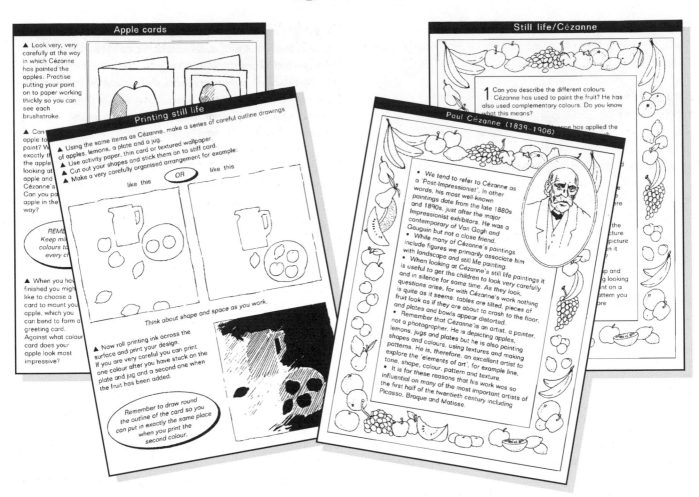

Apple cards

▲ Look very, very carefully at the way in which Cézanne has painted the apples. Practise putting your paint on to paper working thickly so you can see each brushstroke.

▲ Can [...] apple to [...] paint? W[...] exactly th[...] the apple[...] looking at[...] apple and [...] Cézanne's[...] Can you pa[...] apple in the [...] way?

REM[...] Keep mi[...] colours t[...] every ch[...]

▲ When you hav[...] finished you migh[...] like to choose a [...] card to mount you[...] apple, which you [...] can bend to form a [...] greeting card. Against what colour [...] card does your apple look most impressive?

Printing still life

▲ Using the same items as Cézanne, make a series of careful outline drawings of apples, lemons, a plate and a jug.
▲ Use activity paper, thin card or textured wallpaper.
▲ Cut out your shapes and stick them on to stiff card.
▲ Make a very carefully organised arrangement for example:

like this   OR   like this

Think about shape and space as you work.

▲ Now roll printing ink across the surface and print your design. If you are very careful you can print one colour after you have stuck on the plate and jug and a second one when the fruit has been added.

Remember to draw round the outline of the card so you can put in exactly the same place when you print the second colour.

Still life/Cézanne

1 Can you describe the different colours Cézanne has used to paint the fruit? He has also used complementary colours. Do you know what this means?

Paul Cézanne (1839–1906)

• We tend to refer to Cézanne as a 'Post-Impressionist'. In other words, his most well-known paintings date from the late 1880s and 1890s, just after the major Impressionist exhibitors. He was a contemporary of Van Gogh and Gauguin but not a close friend.
• While many of Cézanne's paintings include figures we primarily associate him with landscape and still life painting.
• When looking at Cézanne's still life paintings it is useful to get the children to look very carefully and in silence for some time. As they look, questions arise, for with Cézanne's work nothing is quite as it seems: tables are tilted, pieces of fruit look as if they are about to crash to the floor, and plates and bowls appear distorted.
• Remember that Cézanne is an artist, a painter, not a photographer. He is depicting apples, lemons, jugs and plates but he is also painting shapes and colours, using textures and making patterns. He is, therefore, an excellent artist to explore the 'elements of art', for example line, tone, shape, colour, pattern and texture.
• It is for these reasons that his work was so influential on many of the most important artists of the first half of the twentieth century including Picasso, Braque and Matisse.

Suggestion(s) for extension

Ask the children to do smaller colour still-life drawings using oil pastels. Encourage them to apply the pastels thickly. Roll a piece of activity paper into a tight roll, using tape to hold it together and cut one end into a point as if sharpening a pencil. The children can then use this to blend their colours. Alternatively, use photocopiable page 150 to provide the opportunity to use another medium to explore arrangement and positive/negative space.

Suggestion(s) for support

Discuss the compositions with each of the groups in turn in order to reinforce their understanding of the importance of organising an interesting composition. When drawing make sure that the children work to a good size and recreate the spaces and shapes they see in the composition before them. Photocopiable page 150 can help to reinforce the idea of arrangement.

Assessment opportunities

At the end of the activity evaluate the children's work with them using the same criteria as that applied to the Cézanne work in 'Key background information'. Have they made interesting shapes and patterns? Do their lines vary in intensity? Have they applied colour in a way in which we are able to see their individual brushstrokes?

Note how successful the children have been in recreating what is in front of them, and to record from direct observation. Add to your individual notes on children where appropriate.

Opportunities for IT

Some children might like to extend this work using an art package to experiment with different textures and colours. They will need to have access to the full range of tools and colours. The children should be given opportunities to discuss the advantages and disadvantages of using IT for this work.

Looking at works of art

The Cézanne poster of his work *Still Life with Milk Jug and Fruit* is the focus of this activity.

Display ideas

When mounting and displaying the children's work make sure you check with the children if you want to 'crop' their pictures. Often we look at their pictures, decide there is too much background and use the guillotine to slice off whole sections. In this activity the children have been asked to give very careful thought to their compositions and it is therefore inappropriate to change them without at least asking their permission! Where possible involve the children in any cropping and mounting, giving them a choice of colours in which to mount their work.

Reference to photocopiable sheets

Photocopiable page 150 can be used for both extension or support work. It provides another medium in which to investigate positive/negative shapes and space for extension activities, and provides reinforcement work on how to arrange a still life using a simple medium, so that the children who need support in this area can focus on this skill rather than painting and so on.

Page 151 is used within the main activity and provides an exercise in painting an apple using a technique similar to Cézanne's.

Page 152 provides background information on Cézanne and his work that may help you to further understand his painting.

Page 153 provides a set of questions that can be used to supplement the analysis of Cézanne's *Still Life with Milk Jug and Fruit*.

AN ANGLE ON SHOES

To further develop the ability to record from direct observation. To understand the process by which drawings can be used as a stimulus for further art work. To develop a range of printmaking skills.

†† *Whole class or small groups.*

🕒 *Three or four 60-minute sessions.*

Previous skills/knowledge needed

This activity is appropriate for children at any point within the key stage. It does, however, develop skills learned at Key Stage 1.

Key background information

One of the key areas for ensuring progression in children's art education lies in the growing opportunities given to them to develop their independence. As they learn a range of skills, so they need to be given increasing opportunities to make choices and decisions, using previous learning in new situations.

This activity requires the children to do at least two drawings of a shoe: the first of the whole shoe, the second a close-up of a small area. The children will then be required to develop their drawings into prints. The options that are available include:

▲ A monoprint – produced by rolling water-based printing ink very thinly on to a flat surface, laying a piece of paper on the inked surface and then adding the original drawing on top. The drawing is then 'traced' over, the pressure of the pencil allowing the paper underneath to pick up the ink thereby creating a 'printed' line drawing. (See page 39 for more on monoprinting.)

▲ A relief print – produced by creating a collage interpretation of the drawing using, for example, textured wallpapers, and then rolling ink on to the collage and taking a print.

▲ A line print – using string or wool stuck on to stiff card to recreate the lines of the original drawing, and printing in the manner above.

▲ A rubbing or direct print – taking an impression of the sole of the shoe working directly with the shoe.

▲ A negative print – drawing with sharp pencil on to smooth polystyrene (Easi or Press Print), and then rolling on ink to creative a negative. With this method, texture can also be added by roughening the surface of the polystyrene.

With all these methods the prints can be left with one colour or further colours added by either adding to or taking away from the 'printing block'.

Preparation

Shoes provide an ideal starting point for decision-making. Choose examples with laces and eyelets, so as to provide interesting detail. If possible arrange for all the children to do their drawings at the same time. When completed allow yourself a few minutes to look at their drawings and decide the best way forward. Sometimes you can plan a programme of work and then halfway through find that the next stage is totally inappropriate!

It is best to limit the children's choice as to how to proceed, but it is also useful to have previously looked at the possibilities yourself. You may decide that you require all the children to follow exactly the same processes. However, as you gain in confidence and extend the choices available, so there are real benefits to the children undertaking these different processes chosen by themselves in consultation with you.

Copy photocopiable page 123 for each child, if required.

Resources needed

A range of shoes, paper, pencils or charcoal, coloured chalks or oil pastels, water-based printing inks, rollers, scissors, textured papers, wools and string, Easi or Press Print (possibly lino if working with older children), viewfinders. If required: photocopiable page 123. For extension activity: clay, Mod Roc, newspaper, adhesive, thin card.

What to do

Begin by asking the children to do a detailed line drawing of a shoe. Constantly remind them of the need to look as they draw, asking them questions about the shoe. For example: 'Can you see how the lace comes out of the eyelet?' 'Can you trace with your finger the outside line of the shoe as it has bent and twisted with the shape of the foot?' Urge the children to fill the paper producing a large, confident and interesting drawing.

Follow the first session by asking the children to do a magnified drawing of one small area of the shoe. You may decide to supply them with viewfinders to help them with this task. This time they should colour their drawings using chalks or pastels. Ask them to work with a limited colour range, say blues and greens, and look to add as many tones as they can by the addition of black and white. With this drawing they should cover the whole of the paper leaving no background space. Further drawings may be considered, for example, using pen and ink, including drawing the sole of the shoe. Use photocopiable page 123 if you wish to develop this theme.

Look carefully at the results of their work and now ask them to develop one of their drawings as a print using one of the methods described in the 'Key background information' section. At the end of the session ask the children to share the method they have used with the rest of the class or group. If time allows give the children opportunity to undertake two prints using different methods.

Suggestion(s) for extension

Shoes make an ideal starting point for three-dimensional as well as two-dimensional art work. The children can develop their work either by making a clay model of the shoe they have studied or by working with 'Mod Roc', a plaster impregnated bandage. Alternatively, they may try making a simple sandal using thin card and weaving strips together.

A discarded shoe might also be used as a frame over which papier mâché is applied to create a new form. This can then be painted in bright and glowing colours.

Suggestion(s) for support

Be prepared to support those children who find the drawing difficult. Help them to see how, by drawing a sensitive undulating line, they can significantly improve the quality of their drawing. Poor drawing is often linked to poor observation, and the teaching of art can often be as much about exploring an object with the children as it is about the

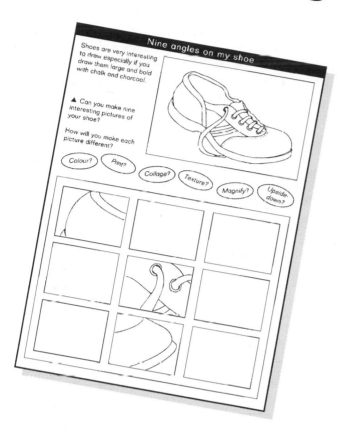

actual act of drawing. When the children are making decisions as to which printing method to use, discuss with them which of their drawings is most successful and how they might be able to enhance this quality when printing. They may need help in making appropriate choices.

Assessment opportunities

Evaluate their work with them at the end of the process. Ask them to explain to the rest of the class or group how they decided on which picture to develop into a print and why they chose a particular process. How do they think they could progress further if they had more time? Where appropriate add to your individual notes on each child, particularly where you consider they are beginning to develop the confidence and skills to make decisions for themselves.

Display ideas

If possible display their artwork with some of the original shoes used in their drawings. If mounting their work use black or a neutral colour rather than a bright mount. Vivid mounting paper often overpowers the art work and detracts rather than enhances.

Reference to photocopiable sheet

Photocopiable page 123 develops the theme of the main activity and provides a visual stimulus. The children are asked to draw nine pictures of the shoe – they may find it easier if you get them to use a small viewfinder which they can place against the shoe in order to decide which sections they wish to draw.

COLOUR IN A CORNER

To develop the ability to select information. To use colour and pattern to create interesting design work.

†† *Small groups.*

🕐 *Three 60-minute sessions.*

Previous skills/knowledge needed

This activity develops skills referred to in the previous activity 'An angle on shoes'.

Key background information

The ability to extract information is an important element of the child's art education. Selecting and organising interesting visual stimulus from which the child can work is therefore a key role for you.

The activity 'Investigating the classroom' on page 17 considered how the classroom should be viewed as an important stimulus. This activity takes this idea further and requires the organisation of a corner of a classroom to create a still life. It uses display as a stimulus for art work.

Preparation

Where space is at a premium it may be necessary to undertake this activity outside of the classroom, for example, in the library or in any other public area suitable for about six children to work comfortably.

The still life needs preparing with some care, but the children should be encouraged to arrange it themselves. Look for very brightly coloured and large patterned fabrics. (Such material is extremely useful and once obtained is worth saving

as a whole school resource.) Large posters can also be included if they are colourful and quite simple in design. (A large Matisse cut-out would be ideal, and these can often be obtained cheaply from cut-price bookshops selling poster books.) Equally interesting results can be obtained by cutting and tearing coloured papers and sticking or tacking these to the wall. Include a table or desk and cover this with coloured papers or fabric. You might also include some interesting items such as a bright parasol or fan. Finally, add a large simple-leafed plant such as a 'cheese plant'.

You will now have created a riot of colour and shapes which the children can work from. The emphasis will be on selecting colour and shapes and recording these to create a flat vibrant pattern. The emphasis should not be on perspective or accuracy of proportion; this would be a hard task for adults let alone children.

Copy photocopiable page 124, making one copy for each group taking part in the activity.

Resources needed

Materials for the still-life arrangement, oil pastels or coloured crayons (preferably not pencils as they do not produce sufficiently strong colours for this activity), coloured paper (for example tin foil, gift wrapping), adhesive, scissors, photocopiable page 124. For extension activity: paper plates and cups.

What to do

Hand out photocopiable page 124 and make sure the whole group can see the arrangement, and can work freely without overlapping papers with the person sitting next to them. Discuss the drawing on photocopiable page 124 with them, noting how the objects are too large for the frame. Their drawings will be much more interesting if they follow the arrangement style on the page, rather than completing a composition in which the objects are drawn small and

'huddled' into the middle of a large piece of paper. Ask the children to complete the activity on the sheet. This will focus their attention on ways in which their work can develop.

Working directly with pastel or chalks, ask them to produce a picture of a main section of the still life. Place the emphasis on working to the edge of their paper stressing that if they work too small they will find difficulty in describing the detail. They should *not* draw in pencil first.

When completed, discuss the results with them emphasising, in particular, the colours and shapes they have produced. Look for sections within their pictures which are particularly interesting, suggesting that they could now select one area and develop it into a larger design. They may find it useful to have a viewfinder to help them.

They should draw these shapes on to a variety of coloured paper, then cut them out and stick them on to a background paper. Their designs can be made more interesting if they create some brightly coloured patterns to add to their designs. They can also produce exciting designs by tearing some of their shapes rather than cutting. As they work they will move away from a faithful interpretation of their original drawing, becoming more concerned with creating new colourful shapes and patterns based upon the original stimulus. When completed, discuss their achievements with them asking them to explain the process they have undertaken.

Suggestion(s) for extension

The children's finished work has validity as a design. They may now repeat one small section or reproduce a very similar design by cutting, tearing and sticking directly on to a paper plate or cup. Their finished collage designs could be cut up for this purpose.

Suggestion(s) for support

In the early stages of their original pastel work be prepared to support those children who find difficulty with the task. Suggest that they start in the middle of their paper and work to the outside, thus concentrating on one small area rather than the whole composition. Similarly, when the children are developing their collages, intervene where you feel they are being hesitant in trying out ideas for new patterns: 'Have you considered…doing a rubbing?… trying wax resist?… using a hole punch to make dots?…'

Assessment opportunities

At the end of the activity collect all the work the children have produced, spending a few minutes looking for evidence of the children's design abilities, and manipulative and drawing skills. Add to your individual notes as appropriate. In this instance you may also consider adding a brief note on the back of their work indicating aspects which you consider they have successfully addressed. Remember when doing this that children who are showing an aptitude for art and design need specific advice as to how they might progress further, as well as those children who are finding difficulty in developing their work. Where you find difficulty in offering this advice then the support of the school's art curriculum co-ordinator needs to be sought. It is not sufficient simply to state 'well done' at the end of each 'marked' activity.

Opportunities for IT

Some of the children could use an art package to work on one part of their initial sketch, using the facilities of the package to create their own style of design.

Looking at works of art

Mention has been made of Matisse. Examples of his 'cut-outs' may greatly stimulate the work produced in this activity, although it is quite possible to achieve high quality results without this stimulation.

Display ideas

If possible leave the original stimulus in place and display evidence of the children's work as close by as possible. Sometimes the children's work can be displayed tightly packed together, but where they have used bright colours and strong designs try to leave sufficient space between their designs for them to be seen as individual works. This may mean changing the display from time to time to allow all examples to be seen.

Reference to photocopiable sheet

Photocopiable page 124 provides a good starting point for the main activity. The children have to arrange their own still life and then make a collage of it using brightly coloured paper they have collected.

A flashy still life

▲ Arrange a group of objects in the corner of your classroom.
Remember to choose things with simple bold shapes.
▲ Can you use your collection of papers to make a big bold flashy collage?

A plant, bowl of fruit and some cloth

▲ Make a collection of the brightest-coloured papers you can find.

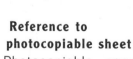

Gummed paper · Coloured tin foil · Sweet wrappers · Gift wrapping paper · Glossy magazines

REFLECTING ON LINE AND TONE

To use line and tone as an aid to recording directly from observation. To develop analytical skills.

👫 *Whole class.*

🕐 *Three or four 60-minute sessions.*

Previous skills/knowledge needed

This activity builds on the children's ability to record with growing confidence from direct observation.

Key background information

While many of the activities in this book involve a sequential series of work in which the children are asked to develop their initial ideas, it is also equally valid for them to produce 'one-off' drawings or paintings in which they concentrate on developing a particular skill.

Preparation

Ideally, you will need to collect one Christmas bauble per child. Again it is worth storing these in school for use in future years. In addition, it is worth collecting a range of other reflective surfaces. Select from brass instruments, hub-caps, bicycle bells, kettles, pewter mugs, school hand-mirrors, shiny spoons and any other items made of chrome or other reflective surfaces.

The first task requires the children to produce a tonal drawing using chalks and charcoal. For this, the children need access to a reflective surface which highlights a variety of tones but does not necessarily offer clarity of detail. In other words the children will be able to select the tones without becoming confused by very precise subject matter. Having chosen the items for them, spend about ten minutes trying the task yourself to check that it is possible, identifying where the children might find difficulty and require help.

In their second drawing the children will be required to look at detail, and this time clarity of detail is very important. In this instance, by far the best results will be achieved using a Christmas bauble. Again it is worth spending one or two minutes gazing into the bauble yourself. Try holding it carefully in one hand and drawing with the other, and you will quickly discover the complexities and subtleties of the task. At this stage you may consider that some of the class would be best to place the bauble on the table, while others hold it in their hand.

When the children are working on this second, detailed drawing, you will need constantly to remind them of one of the most important statements of art, to: 'Draw what you see not what you know!' Repeat it several times, adding detail such as in the reflection: 'How big is your head in relation to your hand?... Can you see your arm in the reflection?... Are the lights and sides of the windows straight or do they curve?... How have you drawn them?... Are you drawing what you see, or what you know?'

This activity also requires the children to work on two scales, fairly large in the first instance but much smaller in the second. Before you start any activity remember to give thought to the size and shape of paper on which the children will work.

Make copies of photocopiable page 112 if required, enough for one between every four or five children.

Resources needed

Stimulus materials as described in the preparation section, grey paper (A3), chalk, charcoal, 2B–6B pencils, fixative, white paper (A6), paints, fine paintbrushes, paper towel. If required: photocopiable page 112.

Still life

What to do

Arrange for each table of children to have access to a shiny, reflective item. Ensure that they can see sufficient reflection to be able to undertake the task. Ask them to do a tonal drawing using chalk and charcoal of the reflection in the item in front of them. The drawing of the outside shape is not important nor is the detail in the reflection. They should concentrate on accurately recording the tones they see. As they work tell them constantly to modify their drawings, adding more charcoal or rubbing back with their hand or a paper towel and adding chalk, until they are satisfied with the outcome. Once their drawings are completed, they will need 'fixing' to stop them smudging. This is best done at the end of the session when the children have left the room.

Follow this activity by supplying each child with a Christmas bauble. Ask them either to hold it in one hand and draw with the other or to place it on the table in front of them. Discuss the need to use a specific pencil or pencils so that they can vary the quality of their lines as they work, pressing hard where they want to show a dark line and vice versa. They should work on a small scale and make sure that they record only what they see.

For a further session hand out photocopiable page 112 and let the children investigate other reflective surfaces.

Suggestion(s) for extension

Working from their detailed line drawings and with constant reference back to the bauble, ask the children to produce either a shaded drawing of exactly the same subject matter or a painting using one colour and black and white. They will need to have access to a fine paintbrush and you may consider giving them a water-colour box rather than the powder colour or 'ready-mix' bottles normally used.

Suggestion(s) for support

Throughout both of the drawing activities it is important for you to ensure an atmosphere in which the children are able to produce their best work. Observed drawing is very demanding. To be successful the children will need to work in almost complete silence, but you will need to stimulate and challenge them by asking the types of questions already mentioned in the 'Preparation' section.

Assessment opportunities

At the end of the sessions select a few of the children's drawings to show to the rest of the class. Pick out areas of success, for example, showing how one child was able to see how straight lines curve in the reflection, or how their hand looks massively bigger than their head. Add to your individual notes, particularly where you feel a child has shown improved ability to concentrate over a long period of time, or where the quality of their mark making has improved.

Opportunities for IT

Children might like to explore the idea of reflection and distorted shapes using a drawing package. With this type of software it is possible to take a single shape, such as a face or hand, and stretch certain parts of the shape to make longer fingers or a squashed face for example.

Children could also experiment with 'morphing' software. In this process the software will automatically change one picture to another in several stages: One face could be changed to another one, or an object turned into a face. Children will have seen the effects of such software on television advertisements where cars or people change into animals. The different steps can be printed out and the sequence put together to form a simple animation.

Looking at works of art

The work of Escher is very popular, especially among younger children, and examples of his work are quite easy to obtain. With a little perseverance you may well be able to find the illustration in which he produced a drawing of himself holding a Christmas bauble. After their efforts the children will find this extremely interesting.

Display ideas

Small drawings need very careful displaying with a good-size border of black or dark grey. They may benefit from double mounting if resources will permit.

Reference to photocopiable sheet

Photocopiable page 112 provides some more ideas for reflective surfaces.

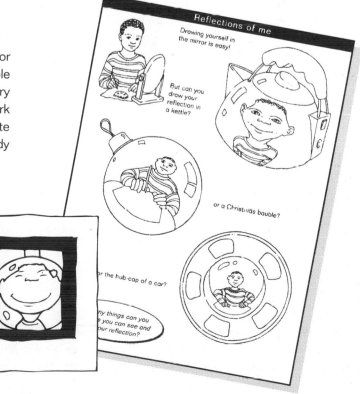

A FRESH LOOK AT FLOWERS

To consider the importance of shape, space and colour when working from plants and flowers.

†† *Whole class or small groups.*

🕐 *Four 60-minute sessions.*

Previous skills/knowledge needed

Plant drawing and painting can be undertaken at any key stage. This activity is intended, however, to be undertaken with children towards the end of Key Stage 2.

Key background information

This activity links designing to drawing. Where possible it is important to show the children that design, art and craft are inextricably linked.

There is no universal way in which an activity should develop. The majority tend to begin with some form of drawing and then progress to the use of other materials. In this activity, the children begin by producing a torn paper collage and follow by producing a directly observed painting. The purpose in working in this way is to 'loosen up' the children. There is a danger when undertaking direct drawing and painting that, as they progress, the children's work becomes increasingly introverted. They take longer and longer over each piece, working in more and more detail, to the point where they fail to finish any of the projects they undertake. By getting them to produce a torn-paper collage

where intricate detail is not possible we can ensure that the children give due regard to shape, space, and colour. They are also likely to produce vibrant and interesting results.

From this they can then undertake a directly observed painting already aware that what is required is not only carefully observed detail but also a considered arrangement of the composition.

Flowers and plants are perhaps the most popular subject matter for art lessons. They are readily available and encourage the children to look carefully. They, generally, then achieve pleasing results . The concern is, however, that each year the children are repeating the same task, with progression coming from the outcome rather than the initial stimulus. It is important, therefore, that the learning objective

is clear on each occasion. It does not matter that the children are returning to the same subject matter, indeed this may be an asset, as long as they are continually developing skills.

Preparation

If the class is to work as a whole on this activity then ensure that there are sufficient plants or flowers. Choose with some care, looking to provide either plants with large interesting leaves or flowers such as sunflowers, daffodils or chrysanthemums, which have a strong, structured head and will be interesting to draw.

Resources needed

A range of plants or flowers displayed in an appropriate vase, black, backing paper (A3), a variety of coloured or white paper on which to paint colours, water-colour paints, pastels as appropriate, adhesive, paintbrushes, rags, mixing trays, water pots. For extension activity: silk painting starter pack and frame, viewfinder, photocopiable page 125.

What to do

Begin by placing a plant, selection of plants or vase(s) of flowers in positions where they can be easily observed by the children. Ask the children to produce a collage on the black backing paper provided. Tell them to tear the shapes from the coloured paper and stick them down. There should be no need to use scissors. Encourage them to consider the shapes not only of the petals or leaves but also those left by the uncovered black paper. They can work to the edge of the paper and beyond, thus producing a large, bold interpretation. Encourage them to work quickly, trying to finish in one session if possible.

Follow by asking the children to do a water-colour painting of the same flowers or plants working directly with colour but without drawing first. Remind them of the qualities they were able to give their collages and encourage them to work freely and boldly. In particular, ask them to 'load' their brushes with paint so that they can paint an area in one attempt, rather than slowly and painstakingly building up the paint with constant need to refill the brush or to remix the colour. Again urge the group or class to complete the picture in one session.

The class now have two pictures from which to work. Ask the children to chose one area from either of their pictures which they consider would best be developed as a stamp design. Working on quite a small scale they should sketch out, in colour, two or three possible ideas. Make sure they consider at this stage where the Queen's head and the value are to be placed. When they are satisfied with an idea, tell them to produce a final neat copy as a collage or a painting.

Suggestion(s) for extension

Photocopiable page 125 is a good extension activity to use here. It provides a link between colour and shape work. The children are urged to use subtle colour changes to enhance their paintings. While it is normally considered good practice to mix sufficient paint to infill the area before beginning, in this instance the results may well be improved by the children needing to mix further quantities of the same colour as they progress. In this way they will produce subtle tonal variations which will give the painting added 'life'. The larger the children work the more interesting will be the results.

Flowers and plants provide an excellent starting point for fabric work. Silk painting starter packs are now available at a reasonable price and two metres of silk will be sufficient for all members of a class to have a turn. To produce a frame, cut a small sheet of plywood or chipboard into rectangular blocks approximately 20cm × 30cm and then use a jigsaw (type of saw with a fine blade) to cut out the centre leaving a 'border' approximately 5cm wide. The silk can then be stretched over the frame and pinned into place.

Tell the children to draw their designs on to the silk and then apply the resist and colours. As long as they follow the instructions and ensure the resist makes a complete border so the colour cannot escape, then success is almost guaranteed. The process is interesting and the results delightful.

Suggestion(s) for support

Spend a little while going over procedures for painting with the children before they start. In particular, remind them how to load the brush with paint so that they are able to complete one section efficiently. Show the children how to roll the brush in paint and then sweep in a line or area of colour.

Assessment opportunities

This activity includes tasks involving three (or four if silk painting is tried) different methods. As well as evaluating the work of the children it is also important that you evaluate the success of the tasks, both while they are in progress and at the end. If a task takes much longer than expected you will need to consider whether to continue with all the remaining sections. Consider also whether the children found the water-colour exercise too difficult, and decide whether you would repeat it another year. By evaluating the activity you can ensure you plan for future progression.

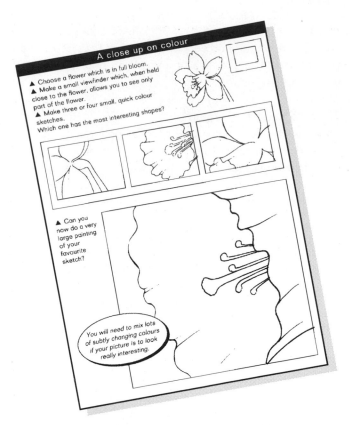

Opportunities for IT

Some children might like to work on one of their pictures using an art package. They could go on to design their own postage stamp, drawing a picture of the Queen's head.

It is also possible to transfer the design on to material using special thermal transfers that can be printed on a colour printer and then ironed on to the fabric. This is ideal for making T-shirts from the children's own designs.

Looking at works of art

Chinese and Japanese artists are masters of producing paintings using the technique of loading the brush and sweeping in colour. Their work is quite easy to come by and you will often find at least one book on Japanese art in the local 'bargain' bookshop.

Display ideas

Schools that invest in clip frames for displaying high-quality artwork demonstrate not only that they give status to the arts, but that they wish to recognise outstanding achievement. Therefore, if the children produce high-quality work consider displaying their work in clip frames around the school.

Reference to photocopiable sheet

Photocopiable page 125 provides a quick colour-sketch activity together with one where the children use colour variations on a large painting. This should encourage the bold use of colour and disperse any worries about using it creatively.

GUITARS, VIOLINS AND TRUMPETS FOR ART

To develop group work and the ability to use the visual elements in picture composition.

†† *Whole class in groups of four.*

🕐 *Three 60-minute sessions.*

Previous skills/knowledge needed

This is an activity best suited for older children in Key Stage 2 and requires the ability to work within a group situation.

Key background information

The National Curriculum requires that children be given opportunities to undertake group work. This activity involves the children planning together, agreeing a method of working, and discussing in some detail to arrive at a final composition.

Normally, we either set up an arrangement for the children, or ask them to organise the objects themselves. Drawing then follows with the children attempting to portray what they see. In this activity, the children are each given one object to draw and paint, before working together to produce a joint composition. For the activity to be successful, careful planning needs to be undertaken by the group. They need to agree at the outset how big each of the items is to be and they should adhere closely to what they decide.

Preparation

Each group will require one item per child to draw. Select from a musical instrument (for example guitar, violin, trumpet), sheet music, a coloured cloth or small table, a potted plant,

a music frame or instrument case. The list can be varied, for example, having two musical instruments rather than sheet music.

Make a copy of photocopiable page 126 for each group.

Resources needed

Items prescribed in the 'Preparation' section, pencils or charcoal, rulers, scissors, paints, brushes, mixing trays, grey or other neutral coloured background paper (A2), white paper for drawing the individual objects, photocopiable page 126.

What to do

Split the class into groups of four. (It is likely to become unwieldy if the groups are larger.) Hand out photocopiable page 126 to each group. The sheet is to be used as a prompt throughout the activity for the children. Supply each group with four main items. You may decide that the sheet music can be added as collage instead of being one of the main items. The group should now decide which item each is to draw, how large the drawing needs to be to fill a good proportion of the final picture and from what angle each item should be drawn. Ensure they carefully follow the decisions they have agreed and ask each child to draw and paint their item. They should discuss colour as they work.

When the group has completed its task (help from other members of the group may need to be given where progress is slow) either introduce them to an example of Braque's work, or ask them to consider how best to organise their final composition. When composing they will need to give consideration to how they are to overlap items, and whether a more interesting arrangement can be achieved by cutting up the objects to create a pattern rather than a formal picture.

(They should see almost immediately that it is nearly impossible to make a photographic interpretation.)

Once the pieces have been moved around and a decision made, then the sections can be stuck down and a final decision made as to whether any further background painting needs to be done.

Suggestion(s) for extension

Still-life arrangements that include musical instruments and accompanying equipment and materials almost always provide very interesting subject matter for drawing and painting. Set up the still life and then ask the children to do three or four, five-minute sketches from different angles. The easiest way to organise this is to get the children to swap seats. This helps them to concentrate on the whole arrangement and how best to organise it on their paper. They can then decide from which position they would like to do their final drawing and painting.

Suggestion(s) for support

Try as far as possible to leave the groups to make their own decisions and to build in their own quality control, checking for themselves that all members of the group are working to the size and colour scheme agreed. The key point for teacher input needs to be at the time the groups are considering their final compositions. At this stage questions need to be raised, particularly if you are not able to show them examples of Braque's work. Ask questions such as: 'How are you going to overlap the items?... Have you considered that you could cut up your objects?... Do you think you should make a pattern rather than a type of photographic picture?'

Still life

Assessment opportunities

Observe closely how decision making is arrived at within the groups. Are the decision-makers able to make good decisions? Are the less able members of the group supported or made to feel inadequate? Add comments concerning their ability to work as a member of a team as well as their artistic progress to each child's individual notes.

Opportunities for IT

The children could extend this activity using an art or drawing package. They could either draw their own instruments or use commercial pictures or clip art, and experiment with different arrangements on the screen. Different backgrounds could be added to make an interesting picture. They could also try cutting the instruments into parts and use these in their picture.

Looking at works of art

This activity works well without recourse to looking at particular works of art. If, however, you are able to show the children an example of one of Georges Braque's still life works before they assemble their final composition, it will significantly enhance this activity.

Braque produced a series of still life paintings in the early part of this century. He was

a close friend of Picasso. For those who do not know his work, they appear, at a first glance, to be a muddle of objects, colours and shapes. They are, however, well worth a long, hard look, and will provide the children with a completely new way of considering their final compositions. They will, at the very least, give them the idea of cutting up their objects and rearranging them on to the backing paper as if they are pieces from a jigsaw put together in the wrong order. More importantly, it will make them consider line, colour, shape and pattern, when arranging the composition.

Almost any Braque still life will suffice, although *The Marble Tree* is an excellent example for the children to study. Some of Picasso's still life works are also worth showing.

Display ideas

Their final compositions will be quite large and worth displaying prominently. If the final outcome is more of a pattern than an easily read picture, then it is worth asking the children to write a short statement about how the work was produced so that others can fully enjoy their endeavours.

Reference to photocopiable sheet

Photocopiable page 126 is a prompt sheet for the children to use throughout the activity.

Landscape

British artists have traditionally been respected for their ability to record and paint landscape. Constable, Turner, The Pre-Raphaelites, and in this century, Lowry, Hitchens, Weight or Goldsworthy are just a few whose work is easily accessible and provides a stimulating starting point for introducing a landscape project. We often associate landscape with countryside but it may equally be concerned with observation of villages, towns, cities, churches, mosques, town halls, schools and factories. Or the weather, observing and recording differing weather conditions. A landscape may include people or not.

Children need to have a number of opportunities to engage in landscape activities. They need to observe and record from direct observation and to engage in imaginative work. Forests, life on other planets, or the world under the sea, all provide good opportunities for imaginative compositions. Looking at the work of artists like Carel Weight or de Chirico will also give them a chance to see how artists can interpret the landscape as a hostile, frightening place.

Be prepared also to offer the children the opportunity to engage in speculation about change. The landscape is constantly evolving and changing, whether it be through the construction of a new conservation area in the school grounds or the building of a new housing estate. Landscape is therefore a good vehicle for introducing the children to 'issues' particularly those which may affect their own lives.

Landscape also allows the children to work as if Impressionists, *en plein air*.

ROOFTOPS AND SKYLINES

To use shapes to create rhythms and patterns. To identify the use of size and colour to signify depth. To develop clay skills including the ability to use texture.

†† *Whole class or small groups.*

🕐 *Four or five 40- to 60-minute sessions.*

Previous skills/knowledge needed

This activity is suitable for children just starting Key Stage 2. It develops work they may have undertaken at Key Stage 1, looking at how colour, shape and texture can be used to express and communicate ideas.

Key background information

Working on activities which help the children come to an understanding of the visual elements is a key component of teaching art at Key Stage 1. This activity extends this idea into Key Stage 2. Understanding and being able to use the visual elements is an essential prerequisite for the children to develop their artistic ability. It is important that in analysing and talking about their work they are able to refer to the qualities of line, tone, colour, pattern, shape and so on. Photocopiable page 156 provides information on El Greco and is a good background to the main activity.

Preparation

The manner in which you plan for this activity depends to a degree on the location of the school, and on the nature of the view out of the classroom window. If there is an interesting skyline with a number of buildings then it would be sensible to use this resource. If, however, the view is of fields or brick walls then the activity will need to be planned as outlined in the 'What to do' section.

Similarly the activity offers a wealth of ways in which to develop the children's initial drawings. Some of these are outlined in the 'Suggestion(s) for extension' section.

Make one copy for each child of photocopiable page 127 and copies of pages 154 to 157, as required.

Resources needed

Photocopiable page 127, paper (try using a long, narrow piece), crayons or paints, brushes, mixing trays, rags, water pots, clay, rolling pins, clay knives, slip, a range of items from which to create textures, poster of El Greco's work *Toledo* (poster in separately available pack accompanying this book, or your own version), photocopiable pages 154 to 157 as required. For extension activity: adhesive, coloured paper, backing paper, card, printing inks.

What to do

Start by pinning up the El Greco poster. Ask the children to explore the skyline. Can they draw the line of the buildings across the sky by using their finger to draw in the air? What type of buildings can they see? What is the shape of each of these buildings? Photocopiable page 157 provides questions to ask the children throughout the activity if *Toledo* is used. Note that while *Toledo* can be used most successfully, you

could use this activity to encourage the children to do some research for themselves, finding a landscape reproduction in a book in the library or on a postcard. Hand out photocopiable page 127 and let the children use it as a useful guide throughout the activity. Whichever landscape they use, ask them to break it down into fore-, middle- and background. This will help them when they move on to the clay work.

Ask the children to think of a building and working draw the outline on sketching paper. Can other members of the class identify it? What types of building have they not drawn? Discuss with them the shapes they associate with churches, factories, blocks of flats, bridges, rows of shops, farm outbuildings, out-of-town shopping centres and so on. Build up a whole range of shapes which they can call upon as a resource for their drawing. You may wish to supplement this by providing some photographs of buildings, and ask them to look on the way home at the various shapes and types of buildings they pass.

Provide the children with some paper and ask them to imagine they are on a hill overlooking a city (refer them back to the El Greco poster) and in the distance they can see four rows of buildings. Starting at the back of the city they should now draw each row, working their way down the paper. Ask them to draw lightly at first as they may wish to make alterations as they go. To begin with they may draw all rows the same size, if they do, refer them back to the El Greco poster. How far away do they think he was from the skyline? How do we show things are at different distances? In this way get them to consider the different size scales they should employ. Continue by pointing out to them that they can also overlap their rows so that a building in the front row may well be taller than buildings in other rows. By constantly asking them to adapt their drawings you will help them understand the need to examine their work critically and make changes where necessary. (Alternatively, you could ask them to do a series of sketches so that they can see the development in their ideas as they add new information.)

When the drawings are complete, ask them to paint (or crayon) their drawings using a very limited colour range. What sort of colours should they use to paint those buildings that are furthest away? Look out of the window, what colours can they see on the horizon? Are they brighter or paler than objects close to? In turn, discuss other rows with them, aiming to help them achieve a final picture in which the rows of buildings appear either to recede or stand out.

The children can transfer their paintings from two dimensions to three. They should begin by rolling out clay and cutting a rectangle to act as the base. More clay can then be rolled out and lines of their buildings cut out. Texture can then be applied and the buildings stuck on to the base using slip. To speed the process you may consider asking the children to work in pairs choosing rows of buildings from both of their paintings.

Both photocopiable pages 154 and 155 can be used for further session work or during the main activity if you see fit. Page 154 explores how El Greco placed his painting on paper. Page 155 shows how buildings and trees go together to make an interesting composition.

Suggestion(s) for extension

This activity has highlighted the notion of developing depth as a precursor to considering perspective much later in this key stage or the next. There is no reason, however, why the children should not consider pattern and texture when applying colour, thereby creating a flat, decorative design.

The picture can be undertaken as a collage with each row of buildings being drawn on to coloured paper and then stuck, in turn, on to the backing paper.

The main activity also offers much scope for printing. The children can cut out the first layer of buildings (those furthest in the background), stick it on to fairly stiff card, and print in a light colour. The second row can then be added over the top and the same colour or a slightly darker one used to print, and so on adding all the rows.

Suggestion(s) for support

The activity does not require a great deal of space prior to the clay work. It should be possible, therefore, to undertake it as a whole-class activity. This will enable you to interrupt the session as you feel appropriate and to make suggestions. It is often a good idea to ask the children to attempt some task without too much instruction and then to discuss outcomes with them. For example, after they have drawn two or three rows of buildings, you might stop them, hold up three or four of their drawings and ask them to comment on their various values. You may comment on the detail of one or the interesting pattern or sense of depth of another. Encourage the children to learn from each other, to experiment and explore as they try out ideas.

Assessment opportunities

Through discussing the children's work with them you will be involved in evaluating their work and making suggestions as to how they might progress. This is, in itself, an excellent way of assessing the children's work in progress.

Landscape

perspective and the completed shapes can be filled with different tones of the same colour using the fill tool. Children will need to be able to select from a palette of colours and make sure that their shapes do not have any gaps in them which would let the colour escape to the surrounding area.

Looking at works of art
The El Greco poster *Toledo* is used in this activity to show how an artist creates depth. Any landscape painting with buildings could be used.

Display ideas
Ask the children to lay their paintings on the floor, then ask three or four children to arrange them in order so that they appear as one long skyline which could travel around the classroom.

Reference to photocopiable sheets
Photocopiable page 127 is a guidance sheet for the children to use as they work through the activity.

Page 154 provides an activity on how paintings can look different if drawn in landscape or portrait format. Page 155 shows the effect of buildings and trees together in pictures. Page 156 gives background information on El Greco and his work. Page 157 provides a set of questions that can be used throughout the study of El Greco's *Toledo*.

Opportunities for IT
The children could extend the drawing activity using an art or drawing package to create their own skyline. They will need to be shown how to use the shape drawing tools and to position their shapes on the screen to create different rows of buildings. The outline shapes can be drawn in different shades of grey to help with the

LANDSCAPE THROUGH A WINDOW

To observe and record accurately from direct observation. To make adjustments in order to work as a member of a team.

†† *Group work – size of group dependent on space available.*

🕐 *Either three 40-minute or two 60-minute sessions.*

Previous skills/knowledge needed
Suitable for children at any point within the key stage. This activity follows on from the previous activity 'Rooftops and skylines' looking at buildings. It does, however, require considerably more advanced drawing skills.

Key background information
Art can play an important role in developing the children's ability to be part of a team. Where a child fails either to concentrate sufficiently or to make the necessary adjustments, then they will quickly come to realise that they have not played their full role in the final work.

It has become very fashionable to ask the children to take a squared section of a famous painting (normally Van Gogh's *Sunflowers*) and enlarge it. When completed all the sections are put together to create a whole. The result is often delightful and the children learn not only something of the artist's use of colour, but also how to work to a very specific brief. The final composite of the children's efforts is often up to two metres square and can be displayed in the school hall or other advantageous place.

This activity is based on the same idea, but instead of cutting up a poster, the children work from observing the view out of a window. The session does, therefore, need some organisation.

Preparation
Decide firstly on the most appropriate window. Besides having an interesting view it also needs to be in a position where the children can see through it easily when sitting on chairs. The more children who can be accommodated, sitting either in a straight line or in two rows, the better. If the window has a number of panes then these can provide the boundaries for each drawing, if not, then use masking tape to create a series of boundaries. (If the children are in two rows ask the back row to draw the view through the upper panes.) Decide how far the children should sit from the window and move up and down the line checking to see the view each child will have.

Make a copy of photocopiable page 128 for each child.

Resources needed
Paper, either A3 or A4 depending on space available and the mural size required, pencils or charcoal, paints, brushes, rags, mixing trays, water pots, photocopiable page 128.

What to do
Hand out photocopiable page 128 and ask the group to work through it with you. First they select members of the group and organise themselves in their positions in front of the window. Explain that they must keep their heads as still as possible. They should imagine they are a camera, and that as they draw they are taking a photograph of the view they see through their section of the window. They should begin by making one or two marks showing where important lines go off the edge of their drawing so that they can check with

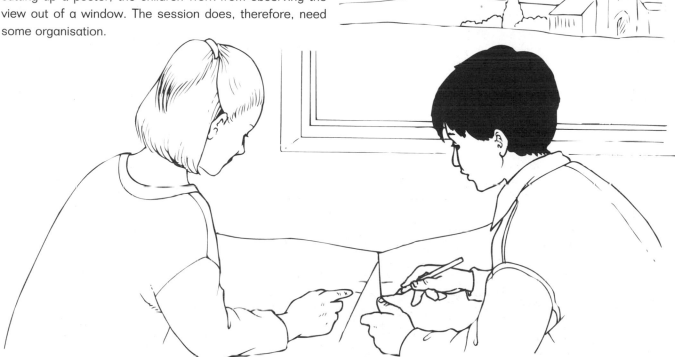

71

ART

the person sitting next to them that they are agreed where these lines are positioned. If they are sitting in two rows they should also check with the person sitting behind them drawing the upper layer. Encourage them to work in silence and to concentrate fully. The task is more difficult than it appears.

Once finished, the children can paint their drawings. When painting, it is not necessary for the children to sit next to the same person as when drawing, although clearly there should be some liaison between all the children as to the colours they are using. Once completed, the views from the window can be laid out on the floor so that the children can judge the results. It is highly unlikely their drawings will match up but it will provide the children with a very good opportunity to compare their drawings with those of others in the class.

Suggestion(s) for extension

If some children finish their part of the mural ahead of the others, ask them to do a drawing and painting of the whole view from the window. They will then see how cohesive one interpretation can be as against that of eight or more individual views.

Suggestion(s) for support

The need to plan carefully and to give precise instruction at the beginning of the session has been discussed in 'Preparation'. Where children are struggling to make the two sides of their picture join up. be prepared to give support. (The younger the children the more difficulty they are likely to have.) This may require you to sit down with the child and make one or two adjustments. At the end no child should be made to feel that the mural 'fails' because of their contribution.

Similarly it should be pointed out to the children that the

objective is not to create the perfect landscape, but rather to show how we all interpret what we see in differing ways. Much of the fun and vitality of the work will come from the differences in the final outcome. The mix between striving for uniformity and allowing for variations is, therefore, an important consideration in deciding how much support to give the children.

Assessment opportunities

You will be able to assess the children's developing ability to record their observations accurately and fluently. This is also true of their developing ability to handle colour. While you will not wish to 'mark' each child's contributions, add to your own notes on the children where appropriate.

Opportunities for IT

The children could experiment with this idea, manipulating a picture drawn by one child, using an art or drawing package. This initial picture could be split into four or even eight parts by selecting parts of the picture and saving each portion to disk. Each participating child can then retrieve a section of the original and enlarge it to fill the screen. They could then continue to work in more detail and add colours to the picture. Each part can be printed out and joined together to make a larger picture. They could even try reducing their portion and rejoining them to make one picture.

The children could try the same idea using a basic pattern outline, with each section completed in a different style or colour scheme.

Looking at works of art

It will help bring the project to life if you can find one of Hockney's 'multiple image photo compositions' to show them. These will approximate closely to the composition with which the children have been engaged.

Display ideas

This work is worth joining together and displaying as a large mural. If it can be displayed close to the window used then so much the better.

Reference to photocopiable sheet

Photocopiable page 128 provides the main activity giving an interesting development on drawing through a window.

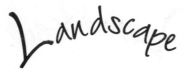

TACKLING LANDSCAPE

To develop the ability to record landscape from various starting points. To experiment with colours and textures to create an experimental weaving.

†† *Whole class or small groups.*

🕐 *Approximately four or five 60-minute sessions.*

Key background information

It is often more difficult to organise activities so that the children can work from direct observation than it is to ask them to work from their imagination or from photographic sources. The benefits, however, are potentially enormous. If the children are to be asked to work from photographs then it is important to be clear about what are going to be the learning objectives.

Recording views of the landscape can be very difficult. To begin with, the children will describe it symbolically, with green grass and green and brown lollipop trees. As the grass comes up to meet the sky in their drawings, so they begin to move from the symbolic to the analytic. It is at this point that they begin to ask questions and become frustrated if they do not find answers. In order to better understand the landscape the children need direct access to it. Learning to draw scenes from looking at photographs is a poor substitute for observing directly. At some stage, therefore, the children need to be given the opportunity to go outside and work directly from nature.

Preparation

In some schools going outside will be easy to organise, particularly if the school is in a rural area, in others it will be more difficult. Be prepared to consider using the school's playing field and any hedgerows bordering it, or a conservation area if the school has one. You will need to decide whether, when using or looking from the school's grounds, there is sufficient information available for you to undertake three tasks with the children:

▲ to produce a colour study of the grasses, hedgerows or trees;

▲ to produce a line drawing in which the children consider the horizontal and vertical lines which make up the particular landscape;

▲ to undertake an exploration of the textures they can observe.

The children will need a clipboard (or similar), and pieces of masking tape to hold down their paper. They should each have four or five pieces of paper on which to record the information. They should use chalks or pastels in this activity; these are easy to work with outside. The 'Suggestion(s) for extension' section, however, lets the children use paints instead.

Make enough copies of photocopiable page 129 for each group, or per four children.

Resources needed

Clipboards (or similar), sketching pencils and coloured chalks or pastels, white sketching paper, simple weaving frames, coloured wools, found items (grasses and so on), photocopiable page 129. For extension activity: paints, brushes, water pots, rags, mixing trays, adhesive.

What to do

Hand out photocopiable page 129 to the children and read through it with them. Explain that they will be producing weavings later, but that they should note how the landscape has been portrayed on the sheet. This will help them to improve their chalk or pastel work.

Take either the whole class or a group to your pre-selected area where they can undertake their drawings of the landscape. Ask them to start by making a series of colour studies of various elements of the landscape, for example looking at the playing field and making a study of the various greens they observe, or looking at the bark of a tree and making an appropriate recording. They may add a few notes as they work. Encourage them to be accurate and to blend the colours until they achieve the desired result.

Continue by asking them to look at line. This is more difficult for they will tend to concentrate on outline. Discuss with them how many horizontal lines they can draw to suggest long, gently undulating forms which describe the humps and hollows across the field or fields (see illustration above). Lines 'in' the field may be long and smooth while lines 'in' the hedgerows are probably more like twisted spaghetti. How many vertical lines can they see, and how best can they record them?

ART

Finally, suggest that they look at texture. What is the texture of the grass? Is it possible to make a series of marks which correspond to this? Tell them to choose two or three other areas and record the texture.

On return to the classroom the children will now have collected a range of information stemming from their observations, which they can use to create their own landscapes. Supply each child with paper and the same materials they used outside. Working very quietly and concentrating fully, ask the children to begin working directly in colour in the middle of their pieces of paper. Ask them a series of questions:

▲ What are you drawing? Is it a tree, a field, a hedgerow?
▲ What colours are you using?
▲ What direction are the lines taking?
▲ What textures are you introducing?
▲ As you work outwards from the centre do you come across a change of scenery – does the field give way to a wood, or a tree turn into a hedgerow?

In this way, by constantly talking to the children, you can encourage them to slowly build their imaginative landscapes, working from the centre of the page to the edges and changing their use of line, colour and texture as they go.

Ask the children to use the same process to create an experimental weaving of a landscape. They can look at photocopiable page 129 again to remind them of how the materials were used to portray landscape. Discuss with them the materials used in the illustration, and ask them if they can improve on this list. In this instance they will need to start at the bottom and work up. Again, however, they will need to think about changes of colour and the way in which sometimes they need to pack down the wool and at other times to leave it quite loose. They should try to build up some

areas with one colour so that the lines do not always extend from one side to the other, but curve and twist. Textures can be added to the weave to great effect by including different grasses or even thin pieces of bark.

Suggestion(s) for extension

Chalks or pastels are easier to take outside than paints. It is important, however, to give the children opportunities to undertake paintings of the landscape. Ask the class or group to experiment with paint to see if they can mix the same colours as they have achieved with the chalks, and to try achieving similar textures. We tend to encourage the children to produce colour washes when painting landscapes. While this is quite acceptable, suggest to the children that they create a landscape in which they apply the paint thickly (adding adhesive to the paint to get an impasto effect).

Suggestion(s) for support

Talk to individual children as they work. One effective way of making the children think more carefully about what they are doing is to take their work away from them, pin it on the wall, and then ask them to look at it from a distance. Ask them which areas they are pleased with and ask them what they think they still need to do. 'If you were to add more...? Have you thought about...? What about if...?' By asking the children questions about their work you will encourage them to realise that the process of making a picture is about making a series of choices.

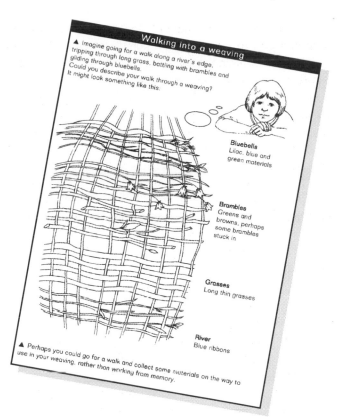

Walking into a weaving

▲ Imagine going for a walk along a river's edge, tripping through long grass, battling with brambles and gliding through bluebells.
Could you describe your walk through a weaving?
It might look something like this:

Bluebells
Lilac, blue and green materials

Brambles
Greens and browns, perhaps some brambles stuck in

Grasses
Long thin grasses

River
Blue ribbons

▲ Perhaps you could go for a walk and collect some materials on the way to use in your weaving, rather than working from memory.

Assessment opportunities

In the same way as discussing the work of a few children with the whole class helps set the agenda for future learning, so discussions with individual children lead to a positive one-to-one assessment and the setting of markers to chart the way forward. To speak to each child individually during each session is almost impossible, however, look for opportunities to give necessary support whenever possible.

Looking at works of art

The Impressionists worked directly from nature and their paintings are regularly referred to, helping children understand the process of drawing landscape. They are not always, however, the best examples. The processes described in this activity could be supported by looking at landscape drawings by Van Gogh, in particular, focusing on the wonderful array of marks he uses to describe the various elements of the landscape. It is more difficult to find examples of the work of Ivor Hitchens but, nevertheless, his landscapes are both challenging and interesting. Similarly the landscapes of Graham Sutherland mirror the idea of working from both imagination and direct experience at the same time.

Display ideas

Try displaying the children's sketches and notes alongside their finished pictures, and, if applicable, their weaving so that other children can see how they have been achieved.

Reference to photocopiable sheet

Photocopiable page 129 supports the main activity and may be used to help introduce the work.

STORMS, SQUALLS AND SUNSETS

To observe and record changing weather conditions. To create imaginative and dramatic landscapes following observations of El Greco's Toledo.

†† *Four groups.*

🕐 *Three or four 60-minute sessions.*

Previous skills/knowledge needed

This activity builds on the first activity in this chapter, 'Rooftops and skylines' on page 68. It requires the children to be able to record, with some accuracy, weather conditions they observe.

Key background information

El Greco (1541–1614) was one of the first artists to paint a landscape devoid of people. Prior to this, artists had tended to use religious subject matter as their starting point, even where their main interest may have been to depict the countryside. Throughout the Renaissance, artists had increasingly attempted to paint towns, cities or countryside,

placing Christ or the Holy Mother in earthly and secular settings. In his painting *Toledo*, El Greco dispenses with the overtly religious setting and concentrates instead on producing an interpretation of his home town, Toledo.

He has been described as a passionate visionary, producing very dramatic work. When considering the painting with the children be prepared to fuel their imaginations and to allow them to speculate on the artist's intentions. Photocopiable page 156 provides more information on El Greco and his work, if needed.

This activity also provides the opportunity to link geography with art, where you can consider cloud formations and look at ways of interpreting them in an artistic manner. Constable was painting at about the same time as the study of the weather was becoming a science. He was, therefore, interested in the study of clouds, in their classification, and their characteristics. He understood not only how to record skies, but their meaning from a meteorologist's viewpoint. You may decide, therefore, to link the understanding of the weather variations with the opportunity for the children to engage in imaginative work. The two often work best when run side by side.

Preparation

Prior to undertaking this activity, arrange for individuals or pairs of children to spend approximately ten to fifteen minutes each day recording the weather conditions. They should observe the sky carefully from the classroom window and produce pastel drawings or paintings. If the children work on a small scale (20cm × 15cm), then on days when the sky is particularly interesting they can concentrate on one small section. They can also be quite precise in capturing the exact colour they observe. As with all observed drawing and painting, check the children's accuracy with them, pointing out, for example, where the sky is slightly lighter or darker at the horizon than directly above them.

Over three or four weeks a whole series of small studies can be collected and used as a source for this activity. Spend a few minutes prior to the first session scrutinising the poster (from the separately available pack that accompanies this book) and prepare the questions that will help the children come to a better understanding of El Greco's landscape. Photocopiable page 157 provides some relevant questions. You may also decide to have other pictures of quite dramatic skies at hand to show the children. As has already been noted, Constable is an artist well worth considering, especially if you are able to find examples of his sketches.

Resources needed

Poster of El Greco's work *Toledo*, pictures and posters of paintings with interesting skies, paints, pastels, adhesive, materials for creating textures (such as sand and paper), sketching paper, activity paper, pencils, charcoal. For extension activity: card, printing inks, white paper.

What to do

If the children have already painted a series of skies showing variations in the weather in earlier art classes, display these where they can be seen and discussed. Introduce the El Greco painting *Toledo*. Allow the children to look in silence and then to discuss the picture. Encourage them to be precise in their descriptions but also encourage them to consider how they feel about the place that the artist has depicted. Ask them questions such as:

▲ Can they imagine walking from where the artist is standing to the centre of the town? Would it be an easy journey?

▲ Do they think the artist has exaggerated the hills and valleys?

▲ What about the sky, do they think it was really like this?

▲ Can they see how the artist has dramatically darkened the sky behind the town? What effect does this have?

▲ When they painted the skies out of the classroom window did they notice differences in the tone of the sky when looking at the horizon?

▲ Because the artist was painting in Spain and not in England would this make a difference?

▲ Try discussing with them the notion of the artist as a 'passionate visionary'. What could this term mean?

Following their observation of the poster ask the children to identify a number of differing occasions when the sky provides a dramatic backcloth, for example, a thunderstorm, winter sunset, squally showers or when shafts of sunlight break through the clouds. Ask the children to select four

examples, and splitting the class into four groups, allocate one particular sky to each group. They should now produce some small studies where they try out varying ideas. Ask them to discuss effects and share any methods which produce appropriate outcomes, for example, working wet on to wet, or mixing wax crayon and water-colour paint.

When ready they should produce a very simple landscape drawing, perhaps doing a silhouette of the view out of one of the classroom windows. Encourage them to have approximately one-third land to two-thirds sky, and to do their drawing on paper which has been cut to a landscape format (the long side of the paper at the bottom).

When producing their final solution you may suggest that the groups introduce collage into their work, adding torn paper shapes to build up the clouds or gluing sand into the sky to provide added texture. They can experiment with these processes by practising on small pieces of sketching paper as they work on the main picture.

Suggestion(s) for extension
The idea of building up the texture can be taken further by asking the children to build up a relief print of the sky. Working on a thick card base they can add a variety of textures using differing types of paper and material or swirling thick adhesive across the surface and then printing on to white paper.

Suggestion(s) for support
Where the children are asked to use their imagination, there is always a temptation for some to work very quickly and without first properly evaluating the results of their initial studies. Working on the final painting is often a far more interesting activity than trying out a number of studies,

particularly for some children. This issue needs to be dealt with sensitively. Two, or perhaps three, studies will suffice. These should be considered with the whole group rather than with individuals in order to ensure they learn from one another and also work with the requisite care and attention.

Assessment opportunities
When adding to your individual notes on the children, this activity offers two opportunities. Firstly, if the children are undertaking colour studies of the weather from direct cloud observations, look for those who show both the ability to observe carefully and make a genuine attempt to record with accuracy. Secondly, when making studies from which to produce their imaginary skies, identify those children who show the ability to develop their studies and make adjustments as required. In these instances look to extend their knowledge and understanding by introducing them to the work of other artists, and by suggesting new or different techniques through which they can improve the quality of their work.

Opportunities for IT
In the initial part of this activity, children could use a computer art package to draw a small section of the sky. They will need to be shown how to select different colours from a large palette (256 colours at least) in order to find the shades of grey or blue they might need. Alternatively, they could try mixing their own colours to create different tones.

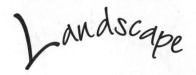

The children can experiment with different line-drawing tools and the spray can to create less sharp outlines. They will need to change the density of the spray, the spray colour and experiment with moving it at different speeds to create dense or outline shapes. They can also try spraying over existing colours to create different textures. Children might want to use the zoom facility to enlarge a portion of their picture to work in finer detail. The children could use these techniques in later landscape pictures.

Looking at works of art

As well as looking at the work of Constable (and Turner) to see how they achieve dramatic, yet accurate, interpretations, look also for examples of the work of some of the Expressionists, in particular Munch and Nolde, both of whom produced some deeply forbidding blood-red skies in their land- and seascapes.

Display ideas

Display various groups' work, showing their four varying sky interpretations. It is also useful to show some of the studies, with brief notes, so as to help explain how the outcome was achieved.

VISITING THE CHURCH

To develop the ability to take notes, sketch and collect information. To identify pattern, shape, texture and colour within a building. To work with a partner in order to achieve a shared outcome.

†† *Whole class visit with paired work. Whole class or pairs on return to school.*

⊕ *One 60-minute session. 120-minute visit. A further 60-minute session.*

Key background information

Art has an important role to play in helping the children to understand better the world in which they live. Undertaking visits or walks around the local environment helps enhance this understanding.

Preparation

Choose either a local church, place of worship or other interesting public building nearby. Make all necessary preparations for the visit, checking where the children may go to collect their information and, for example, where rubbings can be made. Spend a little while exploring for yourself so that you are clear as to which areas you wish the children to concentrate on. On visits outside the school grounds, time is valuable, and a great deal can be wasted by the children wandering around 'thinking' about what they are going to draw. While they will want to liaise with their partner concerning who is to sketch what, it is important that you are able to point out specific areas to them.

The children should each have a clipboard (or similar) when they make their visit and be arranged in pairs so that they can collect as much information as possible.

Prepare targets for them. Will you want them to do three or four sketches each, or as a pair? Will they need to make some notes? Are they to undertake some rubbings from the wealth of textures? Make sufficient copies of photocopiable page 130 to allow a copy for each pair of children.

Resources needed

Clipboards (or similar), sketching paper, pencils, wax crayons, paints, brushes, water pots, mixing trays, rags, oil pastels, coloured and textured papers, tracing paper, adhesive, scissors, photocopiable page 130.

What to do

Hand out photocopiable page 130 to each pair and ask them to complete the activity. Discuss how arranging a composition this way adds interest to the topic. Ask if they can improve on the format on the sheet. Discuss what items they will include in their composition. They can do either one picture between the two of them, or one each. This exercise prepares them for the work to be undertaken in the second stage of the activity.

When they first arrive at the church, spend a few minutes introducing the children to the task explaining the targets you have prepared. The children should start by exploring pattern. Encourage them to be bold in their sketching. Ask them, for example, to look at the patterns made by the pews as they appear to 'stack up' when looked at from one end, or by a row of columns. The more ambitious they are when sketching, the more interesting their pictures will be when they get back to school.

Allow the children about 90 minutes in the building, where they can sketch and collect information. Ensure that they liaise with their partners and collect sufficient 'good-quality' information. On their return to school, each pair should lay out their information and decide how best they can incorporate it into their work. The aim should be to produce a pattern or small mural of the building rather than a photographic interpretation of one specific area (as explored in the photocopiable activity). They need to consider where different elements of their drawings will be placed and how one section can flow into another. This will require them to consider both the shapes they are drawing and the space around the shapes. Both aspects should be equally interesting. A flat pattern should begin to emerge as the pairs work across the surface of the paper. Ask them to complete this design stage of the picture before they begin to add texture or colour.

When they begin to add colour ask them to look at their notes and to remember which colours predominated or made the most impression on them. Do the same with textures. If they produced some rubbings, they will be able to tear and cut up sections and add them to their designs.

Working in consultation, tracing areas where necessary so as to be able to add collage, and trialling different textures and prints, the children can build up their murals.

Suggestion(s) for extension

It is likely that the pairs will take varying lengths of time to complete the task. (Fix a time limit to avoid prolonged extension being required.) For those finishing early ask them to take one 20cm × 10cm section of their mural and to draw it out freehand to the same size. They should then shade in their drawings producing tones which correspond to the colours in the original.

Suggestion(s) for support

Before returning to school, it will be important to check that the children have sufficient information from which to work. Where they run out of interesting shapes as they develop their mural, encourage groups to share and exchange information. Thus, although they are working with a partner, towards the end the children should be providing information into a 'resource bank' from which all can work.

Assessment opportunities

At the end of the activity discuss with the children the relationship between their original sketches and the final work. In particular, return to the issue of whether they collected sufficient information. Identify with them what they have learned about collecting evidence. If, for example, they spend 40 minutes on a sketch, does this ensure four times as much information as a sketch which took only ten minutes? How long should a sketch take?

Where appropriate, add to your notes on each child, highlighting, in particular, progress with collecting and using information.

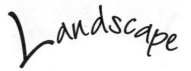

Opportunities for IT

The children could use an art or drawing package to create an ecclesiastical border for their sketches (see 'Display ideas' below). They could take a pattern or design from their sketches, transfer this to an art package (either redrawing it or using a scanned image), add colour, reduce the size and then make multiple copies of the final design. These could then be positioned to make a repeating pattern across the paper. The design 'strips' can be printed, cut out and used as a border for the larger display of their sketches. If children save their design and border strips they can reprint sections to ensure they have enough to go round their display.

Looking at works of art

A number of artists have produced memorable images using the interior and exterior of churches as a starting point. Look for examples of the work of John Piper, a British artist working this century.

Display ideas

Suggest to the children that they produce their own borders to complete their work. Many teachers use templates of letters which are then cut out and used to title displays. These can look even more effective if the children have produced interesting designs to colour in the individual letters.

Reference to photocopiable sheet

Photocopiable page 130 provides an introduction to the activity, preparing the children for the type of work they are going to do.

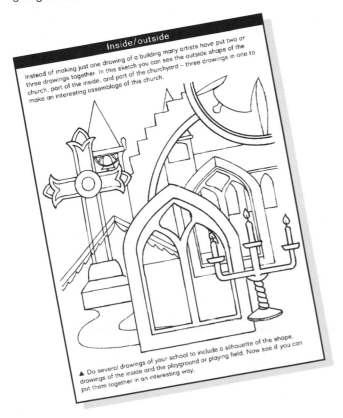

Inside/outside

Instead of making just one drawing of a building many artists have put two or three drawings together. In this sketch you can see the outside shape of the church, part of the inside, and part of the churchyard – three drawings in one to make an interesting assemblage of this church.

▲ Do several drawings of your school to include a silhouette of the shape. Now see if you can put them together in an interesting way. drawings of the inside and the playground or playing field.

THE MODERN LANDSCAPE

To increase awareness of the rapid changes to the environment. To introduce methods for identifying distance including ways of addressing perspective.
†† *Whole class.*
🕑 *Four 60-minute sessions.*

Previous skills/knowledge needed

This activity is designed for those children nearing the end of Key Stage 2. The 'rules' of fixed point perspective are not normally taught until Key Stage 3, although there will be some children ready to undertake this work by the end of this key stage. The children should have acquired competent drawing skills before they carry out this activity.

Key background information

This activity challenges the children to think about changes to their immediate environment. It is aimed at making them question the need for signs and information in and around their school and to consider whether those signs available are in sympathy with the area in which they are placed.

A key task of art education is to encourage the children to discriminate between right and wrong, between good and bad and between beauty and ugliness.

Preparation

Spend a few minutes before the first session checking for yourself the range of street furniture and signage outside the school and within the grounds. Decide whether it is

from school. Discuss with them whether the signs in the illustration correspond with those they observe on their way to school.

At the beginning of the second session decisions can be made as to whether the signage is sufficient, too much or inadequate. The children can also comment on the siting and appropriateness of the signs. Get them to make a series of drawings of the key signs, adding a little background information so as to put the signs in context. You might now suggest they complete the photocopiable activity.

Supply them with a few pictures of motorways or of large city centres so that they can identify the wide range of signs (and advertisements) to be found.

Turn to the El Greco painting and ask the children to consider how different this scene might look today if he were to return and paint this scene again. Encourage them to think about such things as where the road would go. What signs would they find on the road? What other trappings needed to support a major city would they find? Would there be electricity pylons, garages, street lights or large advertisement hoardings?

The children can now redraw the scene adding in the trappings of twentieth-century life as they imagine they might be. This may seem a difficult task, but if you guide them to draw only the main features, they should be able to cope. Alternatively, provide some tracing paper and ask them to trace the main features from the poster and then add the modern day details.

beneficial to arrange for the children to make a short tour of the school's immediate surroundings or whether you will ask them to undertake the task for homework.

Make copies of photocopiable page 131 for each child.

Resources needed
Poster of El Greco's work, *Toledo* (poster in the separately available pack accompanying this book, or your own version) or any other artist's work that includes a road, photographs of large city centres, white paper (A3), pencils, rulers, erasers, ready-mixed paint or water-colour boxes, size 4–8 pointed brushes, water pots and rags, sketchbooks or notepads, photocopiable page 131.

What to do
Hand out photocopiable page 131 to the children and ask the first question. Ask them to close their eyes and consider their journey to school each morning. How many large traffic signs do they pass? On the roadside, within 50m of the school, how many signs do they think there are? These may be either traffic signs, information on the road itself, or on the pavement. How many signs relate to the school? What do they say and what information do they give? Inside the school, how many more signs do they pass before entering their classroom door? If you have made a note yourself before the session you will be able to check their awareness of information that they see around them daily.

Follow by either taking them for a short walk to check the information for themselves or set them a 'homework' task, to check the number of signs they pass on their way home

Suggestion(s) for extension
When working from the El Greco poster, identify those children who have some notion of how to draw items in scale with their surroundings and introduce them to some basic perspective conventions. If you are unclear as to how these principles work, then there are a number of basic drawing books which show this very simply and clearly. Alternatively, discuss the issue with the school's art co-ordinator.

Suggestion(s) for support

When drawing examples of the signs in and around the school, some of the children may find it easier to draw directly from 'life', drawing, for example, the road and adding in all the signs that they observe. The signs may then be coloured to make them stand out more prominently. Alternatively, the children could design some signs for placing around the school, supplying either other children or adults with useful information. Could they also design a more appropriate 'School' or 'No Parking' sign?

Assessment opportunities

Where appropriate note those children who are able to successfully tackle this difficult task, particularly those who follow the principles of basic perspective drawing. Consider saving some of the children's pictures, either to send as part of their portfolio to their next school or to aid you in your report-writing for parents.

Opportunities for IT

It may be possible to obtain an electronic version of the El Greco picture from a CD-ROM or from the Internet. The children could then design their own signs using an art package and import these into the picture; resizing and positioning them to fit the perspective of the picture.

Alternatively, the children could use an art or drawing package to design their own signs for use in the school or classroom.

Looking at works of art

A number of artists have produced paintings of landscapes which incorporate roads. These include Monet, Sisley, Hockney and Cézanne. By looking carefully you may discover a more appropriate image which better matches the ability of your class than the El Greco poster.

Display ideas

Consider displaying their pictures alongside written commentaries the children have prepared, describing the quality and quantity of signs they have discovered.

Reference to photocopiable sheet

Photocopiable page 131 is a stimulus for introducing the main activity of drawing the signs they see on their way to school, and then arranging them into a landscape of shapes.

▲ As you drive, cycle or walk to school every day how many different signs do you see? Can you draw them all? When you go home tonight check to see how many you missed and to see if you made any mistakes.

Sketching signs and symbols

GIVE WAY

40

Patrol

STOP CHILDREN

School

Except buses

STC

▲ Use your sketches to make a landscape of shapes from all the various signs. You may like to overlap your signs and make them look transparent. You may also wish to add cars, people on bikes and parts of buildings. There are many ways you may wish to draw, paint or print a picture of the landscape you pass as you go to school.

Three-dimensional studies

A significant minority of children are able to express their ideas and feelings more successfully when working three dimensionally than when drawing or painting. It is, therefore, very important to include regular opportunities for children to engage in three-dimensional activities. In the past this more or less consisted of a little clay work supplemented by a fair amount of junk modelling. There are, however, a wide range of other materials available to provide a far more stimulating and varied range of activities. These include papier mâché, cardboard, soft florist wire, drinking straws, canes, strips of wood, fabrics and plaster or plaster bandage.

The materials fall into two categories, those which can be modelled (such as clay) and those which are used in construction (the majority). Three-dimensional work is often interpreted as sculpture and sculpture as modelling. It is very important to remember when planning for three-dimensional work that construction activities are equally valid and challenging. It is important to include activities such as crafting jewellery, constructing buildings, making masks, and designing and making stage sets.

As with painting and drawing, so with making and modelling. Opportunities exist for observing and recording the world in which we live, expressing ideas and feelings, and designing and making artefacts which may be either functional or decorative.

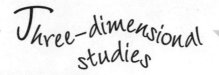

STARTING TO SAIL

To develop understanding of three-dimensional space.
To be able to work as a member of a team.

†† *Pairs in groups of six.*
⏱ *Three 60-minute sessions.*

Previous skills/knowledge needed
Younger children will need help with the technical aspects of this activity.

Key background information
This activity provides a good model for teaching either two- or three-dimensional art projects. It begins by introducing the children to a new skill, encourages them to think carefully about how they use specific elements of art (in this instance colour, pattern and space), and then requires them to produce a solution of their own, working within a tightly constrained brief. Working in this manner, the children are learning not only new skills but also developing their creative talents. Being creative within clearly defined boundaries aids children's development. Where they tend to struggle is when they are given very open-ended projects. The most difficult and often least productive lesson is where the children are given a completely free choice.

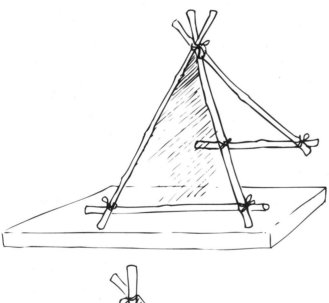

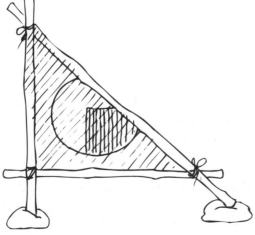

Preparation
The activity requires the children to make triangles with sides of approximately 20cm and to cover them in 'glued' tissue paper. This activity is described using thin canes; however, if these are too expensive or not available, then tightly-rolled paper or modelling straws may be used instead. Covering tissue paper in a mixture of adhesive and water sounds very messy and you might expect the tissue to disintegrate. It does, however, hold up remarkably well, and as long as the children are given assistance should they require it, then very good results can be obtained. As with many of the activities it is valuable to spend ten minutes prior to the session having a trial with two willing helpers.

If canes are used for the frame, then they can be glued together otherwise use sticky tape or thin string. The ends of the triangle do not need to be flush but can overlap as in the diagram (below left).

Resources needed
Thin canes approximately 25cm in length, PVA adhesive, old bristle paintbrushes, coloured tissue paper, scissors, Plasticine or a small amount of clay, a small board approximately 50cm square to display the completed model would be useful but not essential. For extension activity: photocopiable page 132, cup, saucer, shoe, toy, cloth, wool, string, sticky tape.

What to do
Start by telling the children they are to produce a series of simple sailing boats. Each child will make their own although they will need to work in pairs working on one boat at a time. Further, by working in groups of six they will be able to put their 'boats' together to create an interesting sculpture. They should make the two frames, leaving them to dry.

Explain that their sails will be made from tissue paper and that they should bear this in mind when sketching their designs. Working in their sketchbooks or on sketching paper, they should now rough out some designs. The designs should be bold and strong. Tell them to work as if they were putting their designs on to a real boat where they would need to be distinguishable from long distances, and the sails would need to be simple with a minimum of sewing and joining. They should also see their designs as a pair so that, although they do not produce an identical design to their partner, they do look as though the two boats belong together.

The designs approved, they should now cut a sheet of tissue paper which needs to amply cover the triangle. Next, they can paint it with a 50/50 mix of water and PVA adhesive. Working together they can lift the tissue and carefully lay it over their triangle ensuring that it remains as taut as possible. A second layer can be added, if required, to make the sail more substantial. Trimming the edges should not be attempted until the sail is dry. Other pieces of tissue can now be cut and added to create the agreed pattern.

Once both boats are completed they can be stood up, either vertically or at a slight angle, using Plasticine or blobs of clay to keep them in position. The groups of six children can now work together to position their boats in an interesting formation. One idea could be to place them as if at the start of a race when they are all rushing round trying to get to the starting line at exactly the right moment. They will then be seen from various angles rather than in a straight line. If a board is available or if there is a spare area of table or bench where the boats can be displayed for some time, further blue and green tissue paper can be 'roughed up' and spread across the surface so as to create the impression of water.

To finish the activity, ask the children to do a drawing and painting of their finished work. Encourage them to bend down so that they are on the same eye-level and to draw large, bold shapes filling their paper.

Suggestion(s) for extension

Once the children have mastered the technique of building a frame over which they can stretch wet, glued tissue, more demanding shapes can be attempted. For example, if thin wire is used, the frame need not be flat but twisted into a flower petal shape or used to represent a curled leaf. Similarly, a simple three-dimensional form can be built (such as a pyramid) and the tissue wrapped around it. Photocopiable page 132 provides more ideas for this extension. You may hand it out to the more able children and go through the sheet. This can be a very interesting activity if carefully prepared. For example, if the children are given tissue paper with which to wrap the object they will need to be very careful not to tear the paper and great

dexterity will be required. Try to select quite thin wrapping cloth or paper so that the outline of the object shows through. Securing the wrapping with sticky tape may be reasonably simple but not as attractive and interesting as using string.

The more able children may well enjoy experimenting further, either in art club or at other available times during the school day.

Suggestion(s) for support

Try to organise the session so that an adult is available to give a helping hand, if necessary, when they are transferring their wet tissue on to their frame. Check their designs before allowing them to transfer them on to the tissue. Children have a tendency to work small and with lots of detail. They need practice at working with large, bold designs. Similarly, when they are arranging their boats into groups of six, challenge them to look from different angles, asking them whether they are making interesting shapes and patterns from various viewpoints.

Assessment opportunities

Evaluate through discussion with the class at the end of the activity. Ask questions relating to the learning objectives. Ascertain from them which group of boats they think makes the most interesting set of shapes, which individual boat has the most interestingly designed sail and which boat they think is the strongest and best made.

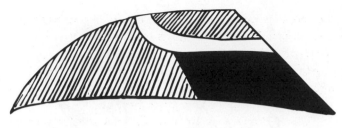

Opportunities for IT

The children could use an art package to design their sails before making them with tissue paper. Once the sail arrangement has been made the children could use their original designs to create an electronic version of the sail arrangement. The original designs will need to be saved to a disk and then imported into the art package. The children will need to resize each sail to an appropriate scale, position them on the screen and then experiment by squashing or stretching their sail designs to create the shapes as seen from different viewpoints of their arrangement.

Display ideas

An alternative to displaying the work in groups of six is to create a class regatta! Assemble all the boats on a flat surface covered with blue and green tissue paper. Two or three children can then be given the task of painting a long backdrop of cliffs, houses and sky as if looking from sea back to land.

Reference to photocopiable sheet

Photocopiable page 132 provides an extension task, involving the children in wrapping complex shapes using similar methods to those they have used to make their sails.

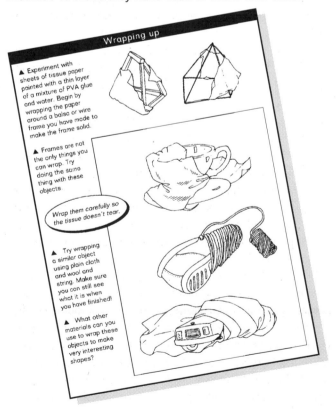

DEVELOPING THE CLAY SCENE

To develop the ability to use clay as a sculptural material. To understand how pictures have fore-, middle- and backgrounds.

†† *Whole class in small groups working individually.*

🕐 *Two 45- to 60-minute sessions.*

Key background information

The poster of El Greco's work, *Toledo* (in separately available pack accompanying this book) is used with this activity. By looking first at the texture and then the structure of the composition the children will develop their understanding of how the artist works and uses the visual elements.

Preparation

Divide the *Toledo* poster up using string, so that there are as many sections as children who are to be involved in the activity. The activity is divided into two tasks. In the first they will be required to recreate their section of the poster as a clay tile in which they have tried to copy and accentuate the textures they observe. Make sure, therefore, that there are enough tools available for them to practise with. For example, provide pieces of lace, bark and fir cones which they can push into the surface of the clay, forks or old combs they can use to 'brush' the surface with and a sieve they can push clay through. They will each need enough clay to make a slab approximately 18cm × 12cm and 1cm thick. The proportions of the clay will need to correspond to the section of the poster otherwise the children will be trying to recreate the poster to different dimensions, a recipe for disaster! Any clay cut away and left over can be slapped together, flattened and used for experimenting.

For the second task, where they will be required to produce a three-dimensional reconstruction of the poster, clay knives will be required if they are to produce high quality work. (This task is not as difficult as it sounds and will provide some very interesting outcomes.)

The groups will have to work in rota for both of the tasks. Provide an area of the classroom where the work will be done. Each group will then, in turn, work there, producing their sections of the poster which you have allocated them. Make enough copies of photocopiable page 133 for one between two children, if required.

Resources needed

Poster of El Greco's work *Toledo* (or your own version), clay (where possible use ordinary clay direct from the bag rather than fibrous, non-firing clay which is more difficult to manipulate), rolling pins, cloth (sacking) on which to roll out the clay, clay knives, wooden struts if available to ensure clay is rolled to a consistent thickness, various items for creating textures and clay modelling tools if available, small quantities of slip (very wet clay in almost liquid form). If required: photocopiable page 133.

What to do

Using clay

To get the best from clay observe a few simple rules. If clay is too wet then the children will find it sticks to their hands and to the table and is difficult to manipulate; if it is too dry then it will crack as the children use it and they will become frustrated. It is best, therefore, to use 'fresh' clay direct from the bag.

Keep unused clay covered in a polythene bag to avoid it drying out.

Hold and handle the clay as little as possible. Let the children feel it, pull it and squeeze it for a few minutes to get

the feel of it. Give them another piece of clay to work with and ensure they leave it on the table, holding it only when necessary.

Ideally, use a piece of sacking or hessian on which individual children can roll out their clay, to prevent it sticking to the table top. When they roll the clay they should roll firmly but without excessive force. The clay should be turned over after each two or three rolls. This makes the task very much easier and again stops the clay from sticking.

Slip is very wet clay in almost liquid form which will help ensure a good join between sections and the base when undertaking the second task.

Make sure that there is an appropriate range of tools available for the children to work with and sufficient for the size of the group.

It is not necessary to fire the children's clay work at the end of the session but if you do have access to a kiln it is worth using. Fired clay work greatly enhances the work and will allow it to be painted using either paint or felt-tipped pens.

Allocate each child one section of the poster and a ball of clay. Encourage them to familiarise themselves with the feel of the clay and its properties.

After experimenting they should work carefully to recreate their section of the poster in the clay using as many different textures as necessary. This can be achieved by pressing into the surface using a variety of different objects and by building up the surface by adding further layers of clay. Encourage them to be bold. They should create a finished tile where there is a wide range of textures and depths.

On completion the tiles can be brought together and the children can make a few small adjustments to give the finished work some semblance of cohesion.

Follow this task by asking the children to roll out another slab of clay, larger than the first, from which they cut a square approximately 15cm × 15cm. This can then be used as the base of the model.

Working on a strip of clay, the child should now decide on the foreground of the scene on the poster and draw this on to the clay. For example, this may be thought to be a line that runs around the top of the trees on the right, swooping down below the river, and then finishing on the left by going up and over the foreground tree. This shape can then be cut out, textures added and when complete, stood up, stuck using slip and modelled on to the front of the base square.

The middleground may now be added in the same way, this perhaps including some of the buildings on the right and working along the wall, turrets and bridge which form the boundary to the town. Again, this can be textured and then added to the centre of the square base. (Remind the children that as they work on this section they need to build the panel slightly higher than the first.) They can now add the background panel, working their way across the skyline.

ART

These instructions may sound rather complex but you will find that the children quickly understand the task and will need little advice. Allow them as much scope as possible for deciding how they are to structure the sections.

If the children have responded well to the second task, use photocopiable page 133 to continue this type of work in further sessions. This is suitable for paired work. Tell the children to experiment before beginning the final work to see what textures they can produce. Leave them to complete their models, letting them decide on the type of town it will be, and how it will be laid out.

The town on the hill

1 Roll out a slab of clay and lay it over an upturned saucer. Do not cut off the overlapping pieces.

2 Now make some small blocks to be your houses, factories and churches. Using a small modelling tool, press in the windows and doors and add a roof.

3 Make small balls of clay. Press a small amount of clay through a sieve and add this on to three balls to make bushes and trees.

4 Begin to construct your 'town'. Press in the paths and use small pieces of bark to press on to the base to make the textures of fields.

You may find it easier to work with a partner.

Suggestion(s) for extension

This activity is based on the El Greco poster. Other paintings can be used in the same way. Children who show an interest in working with clay, and successfully complete this activity, may be encouraged to choose a favourite painting from which to work and build up the three basic sections in more detail. This may include working with curved sections running diagonally as well as directly across the base. Cézanne's work, *Still Life with Milk Jug and Fruit*, could provide an interesting alternative to modelling a landscape.

Suggestion(s) for support

Where children have difficulty identifying the fore- and backgrounds, ask them to trace over the poster, working with three lines going from one side to the other. If necessary they can then lay the tracing paper on to the clay to act as a template. It is important that the children make a good start. If the clay slabs are of uneven thickness then the task will be made much more difficult. Check the quality of their rolling, therefore, before allowing them to continue further.

Assessment opportunities

As with all art, high quality craftsmanship is central to producing interesting, stimulating work. Discuss the quality of their work looking at how well they have joined the clay slabs together, the quality of their cutting and the manner in which they have smoothed and finished their models. Add to your individual notes where you identify work of a particularly high standard.

Looking at works of art

Any landscape is appropriate for this activity although, whichever is used, it is advisable to check with the child before they begin, so as to be clear how they intend to construct their model. The Cézanne still life provides an equally interesting starting point and, for older more able children, a real challenge to produce a full three-dimensional interpretation.

Display ideas

The finished models are best displayed near or on children's eye-level. Display, if possible, on a shelf where they can be seen but not touched unless they have been fired. Preferably do not paint them as this will detract from the texture.

Reference to photocopiable sheet

Photocopiable page 133 can be used for further sessions working with clay. It provides a similar activity to the main task, but allows the children to use their imaginations and decide on a town themselves, rather than using a stimulus.

EXHIBITING CLARICE

To develop the ability to display products in an interesting way.

†† *Paired work organised into small groups or whole class.*

🕐 *Three 45- to 60-minute sessions.*

Key background information

The link between design and technology and art can often appear very blurred, particularly when working three dimensionally. As a rule of thumb, it is likely that if the task is primarily functional then it may fulfil the requirements for design and technology, if primarily aesthetic then it meets art criteria. This is, however, a fairly sterile argument. Tasks of this sort can often meet the demands of both subjects and this is, therefore, a useful cross-curricular activity.

Very early in the activity the children will be required to design their exhibition stand. The temptation is to do this as a paper exercise, first drawing their stand two dimensionally and then making a model from their drawings. While this can be a useful exercise, it is also extremely difficult and can be time-consuming and non-productive. When designing, be prepared to let them experiment with the materials at their disposal, tell them to hold them up and, without fixing, try to get a feel for how the materials might go together. In other

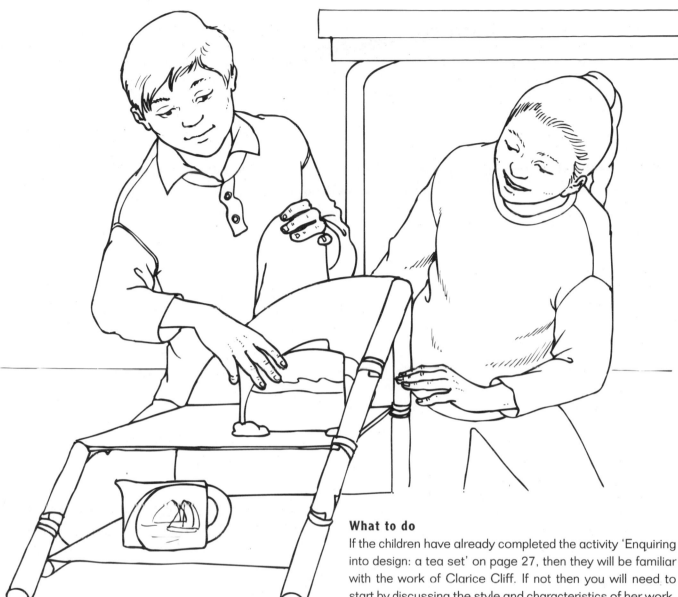

words, allow them to design three dimensionally, rather than having recourse to two dimensions first.

Preparation

The exhibition stand can either be made to life-size or smaller, depending on the quantity and quality of the materials made available to the group or class. Ensure that there is a sufficient range of drinking straws and card available if small models are to be made, and thin cardboard tubes if the models are to be of a practical size.

For those children who finish successfully, you may decide to copy photocopiable page 134.

Resources needed

Modelling straws or thin cardboard tubes, card, adhesive, scissors, pencils, coloured papers, sticky tape, paints, brushes, water pots, poster of Clarice Cliff's work *Bizarre* (poster in separate pack accompanying this book, or your own version). If required: photocopiable page 134, pencils.

What to do

If the children have already completed the activity 'Enquiring into design: a tea set' on page 27, then they will be familiar with the work of Clarice Cliff. If not then you will need to start by discussing the style and characteristics of her work. Point out that the poster displays three sets of ceramic work and ask them to discuss the merits of each. Which do they prefer? In this poster the work has been photographed against a plain, black background, but if it were displayed in a shop how could it be shown to best effect? Explain to the children that it is the task of some people to design exhibition stands. If they had to design a stand for this work what would they have to consider and how would they go about it?

Depending on the range of materials at your disposal and the ability of the children, ask them, working in pairs, to choose one of the three sets of crockery and design a small stand on which to display or exhibit it. Their stand should mirror the style of the crockery. For example, if they prefer the central flower-patterned set, then their display stand could have the shapes as the base, and the colours used in the flowers stuck on to the supports or twisted around them. Similarly, the set with the abstract design could incorporate strong zigzags.

If working to a large scale using cardboard tubes, then their final model should be sufficiently large for them to display

two paper plates and cups, decorated and painted in the appropriate style. If working with drinking straws then they may simply draw a plate and teapot to the relevant size, colour them and cut them out, and then prop them in position within their display.

Those children who have finished the first activity successfully could then make a pencil box. Hand out photocopiable page 134 and discuss the various questions. Let the children do the task on their own, but be prepared to lend any support needed. If they perform this task well, let them make a box in which to package a cup and saucer, where the design mirrors the style of the crockery.

Suggestion(s) for extension
Those finishing early may consider how they would include a display board with the words 'Bizarre' by Clarice Cliff'. To do this they might try to find examples of typefaces used in the 1930s.

Suggestion(s) for support
The children will need advice when putting the various elements together and should discuss their ideas before beginning. When introducing the activity it is worth spending some time with the whole class before they start. This will enable you to discuss some of the possibilities, as well as explaining how they might make the stand.

Assessment opportunities
At the end of the session decide with the group or class the criteria they would use to evaluate the finished work. For example, they might consider which is the most eye-catching, which is the best made and which is closest in style to the crockery. They can then try grading the results using their criteria and working with a 1:5 scale. They could also consider how their designs might be improved.

Opportunities for IT
The children could use a word processor to make the label for their display stand. They could experiment with different fonts to create a 1930s style print. They will need to be able to select from the range of fonts available, or even use fonts from another disk or CD-ROM not normally available on the computer they use. The children could also use the text facility within an art or drawing package to create the same effect.

Looking at works of art
The poster of Clarice Cliff's work *Bizarre* is used in this activity.

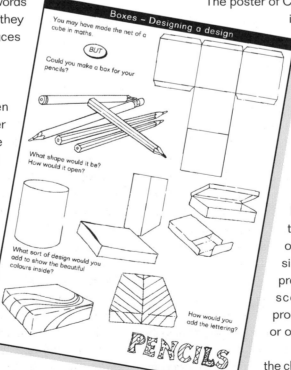

Boxes – Designing a design

You may have made the net of a cube in maths.

BUT

Could you make a box for your pencils?

What shape would it be? How would it open?

What sort of design would you add to show the beautiful colours inside?

How would you add the lettering?

PENCILS

Display ideas
Exhibiting the children's display stands requires some thought! They may be best as in the poster, displayed against plain, black paper or cloth.

Reference to photocopiable sheet
Photocopiable page 134 allows the children to design the shape of a box for themselves, rather than simply following the directions to produce a cube. It also gives them scope to use lots of colour, producing either an abstract design or one incorporating illustrations.

Make sure that you encourage the children to consider their decisions carefully before undertaking the work.

UP AGAINST THE WALL

To develop clay modelling skills. To produce an imaginative response to a specific brief.

†† *Whole class or small groups of four or five.*

⏱ *Three to five 60-minute sessions.*

Previous skills/knowledge needed

This activity requires the children to model quite fine detail and to work from their drawings. It is therefore most suited for children near the end of Key Stage 2.

Key background information

Expecting children to work directly from their drawings and interpret them accurately is to set a very demanding task. By getting them to draw first, allows them to consider how the weight of the body falls and to look at the proportions of the figure. They can then use these drawings as reference, when modelling.

It is a requirement of the National Curriculum that the children learn to investigate and record their observations prior to producing their own response. Through working in this way they are following the best practice used by sculptors throughout the centuries. However, photocopiable page 135 provides an alternative starting point which you could use to highlight how the main activity is going to be done.

Preparation

The children begin by drawing classmates posed either leaning against the back of a chair or bending over it. Prior to the lesson check that a firm, stable chair of the correct height (approximately waist-high to those children who are to pose) is available or, alternatively, use a table. Ensure that the children will be able to see the whole of the pose. It would be best if the children were in small groups. These are more manageable, allow all the children to see, and mean that the child posing has the opportunity to draw if the work is done on a rota basis. If the whole class is to be involved then the drawing may need to be done in a large, open space with the children working on the floor. You could use a wall for the children to lean against, but, although this is safer and easier to do, not so many children will be able to see and, therefore, draw.

When they model figures working from their drawings, they will need access to clay that is either direct from a new bag or has been fully reconstituted. They will also require proper clay modelling tools in order to show fine detail.

Decide whether you are going to use photocopiable page 135 first. The mask provides an alternative starting point. Sometimes it is advisable to give the children the clay and ask them to design as they proceed; at others they should sketch their designs first as described in the 'What to do' section below. In this activity, if the children work in groups at differing times, you may try both methods and then compare outcomes with them, on completion of the project.

Make enough copies of the photocopiable page 135 so each child has one, if required.

Resources needed

Wall, table or stable chair, four sheets of drawing paper, 2B pencils, drawing or clipboards if working on the floor, clay, sacking or newspaper, a wide range of modelling tools, wood, strips of balsa, lollipop sticks or other suitable material to make a wall or fence approximately 8cm high and 20–25cm long. If required: poster of Lowry's work *The Playground* (this is in the separately available pack accompanying this book, or use your own version), photocopiable page 135, round or oval plate, talcum powder, books on African masks and so on. For extension activity: paints and brushes.

What to do

During the first session ask the children to undertake four, ten-minute drawings of a classmate posed either leaning against or propped up by a chair, table or wall. Ask them to decide on the pose. (As a starting point you could refer to the Lowry's painting, *The Playground* and point out the man to the right of the picture, halfway up the steps who is leaning over the fence and staring out.) As the children draw, point out how the weight of the figure is spread, the angle the figure takes and the height of the body against the top of the 'wall'. Ask the children to move their position after each drawing so that they see the pose from a variety of angles. If this is not possible then try to move the angle of the table or chair. After each pose, discuss several of the drawings so that the whole class or group can see how different the pose looks from different angles.

The wall or fence should be made prior to modelling the figures. If made from wood then the poles can be pushed into lumps of clay to make it sufficiently stable to pose the figures against.

Display a wide range of the children's drawings so that they have different references from which to work, not just their own. They will need to roll out a fairly thick coil of clay for the body and a thinner one for the arms and legs. Overall, the figure, if standing upright, should measure approximately 15cm in height. The children should join the coils using a modelling tool to ensure good joins. (A little slip could be used as a cement, but if the clay is in good condition and the children have not handled it too much then this should not be necessary.) Check that the figures have been 'well made' and then ask them to bend their figures into the position they desire, either in front or behind the fence. Further detail can be added, turning the figure into a: football supporter, child in the playground or person queuing at a bus stop. To clothe their figures, clay can be pressed very thinly and then added over the top of the coil.

To finish the scene, the children can set their figures in groups of four, five or more. (The wall or fence can be extended as far as necessary so that all the figures can be part of the same tableau.) The finished work will be greatly enhanced if the figures can be fired and then glazed. If not, then leave the figures in their natural state; it is unwise to try and paint them.

Suggestion(s) for extension

Working from their completed model ask the children to draw their finished group of clay figures. If they have not been able to fire and glaze their three-dimensional models then they can paint their drawings, thereby showing more detail. Ask the children to work large and fill the paper – their drawings should be at least the size of their clay figures.

Suggestion(s) for support

Be prepared to support the children where necessary. As with all activities it is useful to continually challenge them to add more detail, refer back to their drawings, look at the work of others in the class and to stand back and look at their model to check they are achieving their original intention.

Clay masks

▲ Begin by rolling out a slab of clay and laying it over a large round or oval plate. Sprinkle talcum powder over the plate before beginning so it doesn't stick.
▲ Cut off the overlap.
▲ Using the strips made by the overlap, cut out large eyes, nose and mouth to make very strong simple shapes.

▲ Add these features to the base using some slip (very wet clay) to act as glue.
▲ Work the eye into the base using a modelling tool to get a secure fix.
▲ To make your designs interesting look at pictures of Sri Lankan curing masks. Japanese Nō theatre masks and traditional African masks.

Assessment opportunities

This activity offers the opportunity to assess the children's development in both drawing and modelling. At the end of the task discuss how they feel they have completed the work – where they have been particularly successful and where they might improve the work. Add to your individual notes as appropriate.

Looking at works of art

The poster of Lowry's work *The Playground* can be used as a visual stimulus to show the type of stance they are attempting to achieve in their modelling.

Display ideas

This activity offers good display opportunities. Try to show the three-dimensional work alongside their drawings and, if undertaken, their paintings of the finished models.

If the models have not been fired and glazed then they should be placed against a plain, black background so that they can be clearly seen. If the models have been painted, the children could paint a background scene in keeping with the model theme.

Reference to photocopiable sheet

Photocopiable page 135 provides an alternative starting point. The children design as they make, rather than sketch ideas from which to work – as in the main activity.

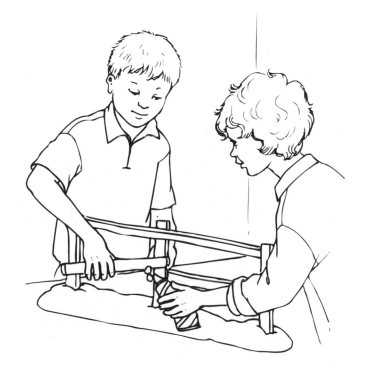

 BRIDGE FOR ALL SEASONS

To develop understanding of symbolism using colour and shape. To develop constructional skills.

†† *Small groups or whole class, working in pairs.*

🕐 *Three 60-minute sessions.*

Previous skills/knowledge needed

The activity requires cutting and sticking skills and is suited to children in the middle years of the key stage.

Key background information

This activity gives children the opportunity to experiment. When designing and making their bridges they will need to experiment with and use the visual elements, experiment with and develop control of tools and techniques, and experiment with ideas for their work. By giving the children a specific brief and by ensuring they work through a series of set tasks, the experimentation takes place within a defined context and allows them to evaluate progressively their achievements.

Preparation

Ensure that an appropriate range of materials are available. You will need card that can be cut but is sufficiently thick not to curl up when painted and stuck on to a frame. You may need one copy of photocopiable page 136 for each pair of children if further sessions are to be undertaken.

Resources needed

Stiff white, grey or appropriately coloured card, scissors, rulers, pencils, sketching paper, paints or pastels, drinking or modelling straws, floristry wire, PVA adhesive and collage materials as appropriate. If required: copies of photocopiable page 136, one for each pair of children.

What to do

The children, working in pairs, are to produce a bridge of any design, for example, an arch, an 'H' shape or triangular. It may be for cars, trains or pedestrians, but in scale it should be of sufficient size to span 15cm. The bridge is to be bright, colourful, very decorative and built on a theme representing one of the seasons.

Start by asking them to choose a season and then select four colours which they think best suit that season. They should work with their partner both trying out colours but then decide from perhaps eight or ten colours which they feel are most appropriate. Similarly, they should try out a series of shapes. This is rather more difficult and some discussion may be necessary. Encourage them to go for shape rather than objects. For example, leaves could represent autumn, but they will get more interesting results if they decide on twisting, curling shapes as well, which could be said to represent smoke from a bonfire. There could be some fruit or berry shapes (round and smooth) acting as a contrast. Groups working on the theme of spring or summer should work through the same process. Be prepared to challenge the children with their choice of shapes and colours.

The shapes and colours chosen, the pairs can now decide on the shape and structure of their bridge and proceed with the making. It is easiest if it is constructed using straws which are glued and taped or tied together (like scaffolding). While the children are waiting for it to dry they can begin to draw, cut out and paint (if not using coloured card) their shapes, having first decided where they are to fit. In this way the shapes fulfil a decorative role and are not part of the structure itself. Other collage materials can be added if you wish. The shapes can then be stuck into position and the bridges completed.

In a further session, hand out photocopiable page 136. Go through the fundamental design questions with the class and then leave them to research and make their decisions. Discuss these once the children are ready and then, if time allows, ask them to make their models.

Suggestion(s) for extension

This extension idea is one that needs to be decided on at the start of the main activity. The more able children may wish to make their shapes form part of the structure rather than adding them on at the end. If they are to work in this way then they ask them to produce a very small model to start with so that they can see how the shapes fit together. Thin floristry wire can be used to enclose parts of the bridge; tissue paper, coated with a thin layer of adhesive and water, can then be laid over the wire to decorate it.

Suggestion(s) for support

You may find it useful to read the children a poem or passage from a book in order to stimulate their imaginations. Share good ideas and get some of the pairs to talk about their work as they proceed, so as to stimulate others. Give practical assistance where required when the children are in the process of constructing. Do not, however, choose the shapes or colours for them.

Assessment opportunities

Talking about the work as it proceeds enables regular assessment to be made and changes introduced where necessary. If you are going to assess the outcomes with them then it is useful to have agreed the criteria at the outset. For example, suggest that at the end of the task all the children will take part in the evaluation deciding who has made the strongest bridge, who has the most interesting shape and whose bridge best represents the season chosen. They should be prepared to state the reasons for their choice.

Opportunities for IT

The children could use a drawing package to help them with the initial design of the bridge. They will need to be able to draw shapes such as rectangles and triangles, copy and resize them and move them to different parts of the picture. They may also find it useful to be able to rotate or flip their shapes so that they can use the same shape on both sides of their bridge. This will give them an opportunity to experiment with their design before starting to make the bridge.

The children could also work on the seasonal colour scheme by selecting a range of tones from the colour palette. These could be used on a second drawing showing the decoration of the bridge. The children can ensure they have a decorated and undecorated copy of the bridge by saving a copy of the first design, retrieving it, adding the decoration and then saving it with a different file name.

Looking at works of art

The Goodwill Art Service publish a pack of postcards based on the theme of bridges. It is a subject matter often used by artists and, while the bridges shown on the postcards may not be of direct relevance to this activity, they provide a number of interesting possibilities for further extension work.

Display ideas

Cardboard boxes of varying sizes, stacked together and covered with cloth, provide a good base on which to display the finished bridges. Ask the children to write a short description of their bridge, outlining how they made their decisions and what problems they encountered while working.

Reference to photocopiable sheet

Photocopiable page 136 provides a similar activity to the main task, and could be used in further sessions with children who show enthusiasm in the initial task. They have to design a tower for a special occasion. The sheet asks important design questions which the children would have to consider for any design task of this nature. The activity is suitable for pairs of children to work on.

Be aware that this is an activity where work of varying complexity may result. The open-ended approach requires support if good results are to be achieved. It is best, therefore, if the children are closely supervised. They may also need help in collecting appropriate materials, although they should be given every encouragement to find the materials themselves. It is best, if possible, for them to work in groups of six with adult support.

Preparation

Prepare objects capable of being incorporated into sound sculptures, for example, tin cans, small bottles (glass and plastic), metal objects, cardboard boxes, cling film, greaseproof paper, elastic bands, small pebbles and tiny stones. The objects may fit into a number of categories including those which can be shaken, banged, twanged, blown and rolled.

Resources needed

Paints, adhesive, paper, brushes, water pots, newspaper, 'musical' objects (see 'Preparation'), photographs of musical instruments from around the world.

What to do

This activity requires the children to work individually to make a noise machine which is going to play a part in a musical arrangement. Discuss with them, prior to the first session, the various possibilities. Begin by asking how they might go about making a noise machine (or musical instrument) which needs to be shaken to activate the sound. Continue by discussing other methods. Explain that they need to find objects and materials which they could use to make a particular sound.

MAKING MUSIC

To gather resources and materials to stimulate and develop ideas.

†† *Groups of six.*

🕐 *Two or three 60-minute sessions.*

⚠ *The children need to be made aware of the health and safety issues surrounding dirty 'objects'.*

Key background information

In the vast majority of activities, particularly at Key Stage 2, the onus is on you to provide the stimulus for the lesson. It is, however, a requirement of the National Curriculum that the children collect information and items themselves for use as artistic stimuli.

Some of the greatest artists succeeded through their ability to scavenge, sort and uncover objects and items that are either directly used in their art work or provided the starting point for drawings and paintings. For example, Henry Moore often used stones, pebbles or bones as the starting point for some of his most memorable sculptures.

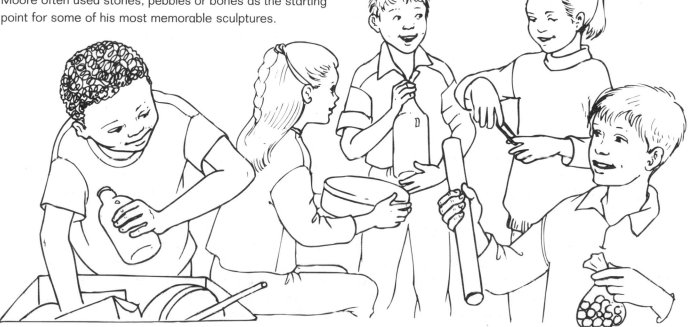

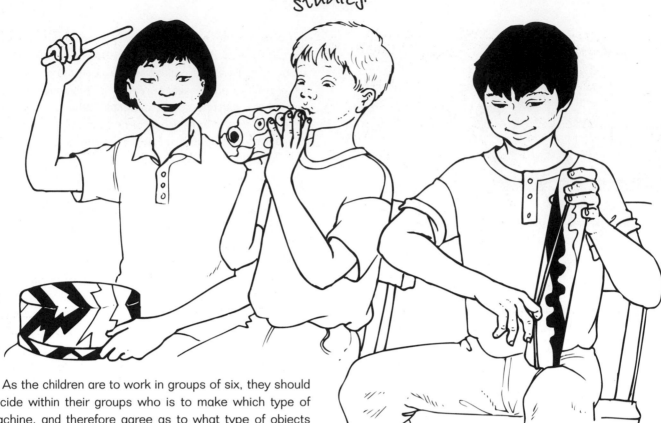

As the children are to work in groups of six, they should decide within their groups who is to make which type of machine, and therefore agree as to what type of objects they need to collect. They should also discuss how the end results will come together in a musical arrangement. It will be necessary to discuss health and safety issues with them – carrying glass bottles or rusty cans to school will not be appropriate.

The task of making the machines should be undertaken in two parts. The children should first complete the functional task ensuring that, when completed, their machine works. They can then consider the decoration. When decorating ask them to produce lively, vibrant interpretations, using bright colours and strong shapes. With older children ask them to consider shapes and colours which correspond to the noise their machine makes. They will also need to decide on the correct materials and paints for the task. You could show them pictures of musical instruments, both from their own and other cultures, so that they can see the care taken in the making process.

When completed the groups can produce a 'musical arrangement' to demonstrate how the noise machines they have created work.

Suggestion(s) for extension

This task can be organised to suit the ability of the child. The more able children should be encouraged to make quite complex instruments whereas the less able can make simple percussion instruments. In order to complete the task the children creating complex instruments may need to work at other times of the day. Rather like Leonardo da Vinci (or Heath Robinson!), the children who show an aptitude should be encouraged to design machines which they might not be able to make but which demonstrate interesting ideas.

Suggestion(s) for support

By working in small groups the children can be encouraged at each stage to try out ideas, practise designs and gain technical support where they find difficulties. When designing, ask them to consider working as a team, for example, all using the same colours.

Assessment opportunities

At the end of the task, the children can describe their musical instruments or noise machines to the rest of the class and then demonstrate how they work. When the group has done this and then played their arrangement, the class can provide their own evaluation. While this activity is in progress, add to your notes on individual children.

Looking at works of art

Jean Tinguely, a twentieth-century sculptor, has created a wide range of strange machines that make noises, jump up and down and spew out balls or bubbles. Although examples of his work may be a little difficult to come by, you may find relevant photographs or prints. Be prepared to show the children photographs of musical instruments from around the world so that they can discover the detail and care which goes into the decoration.

Display ideas

Many schools have posters of musical instruments, either representing the instruments of the traditional orchestra or showing instruments from other cultures. These would make an interesting backdrop for the children's own efforts.

Design

'Design' is a much-maligned word used both by artists and technological craftsmen but often in very different contexts. To the technological craftsman design is that activity which enables or informs making and is often, but not always, undertaken prior to making. At times, as with designing a piece of fabric, the designing and making may be inextricably linked. For the artist, designing is much broader and may refer to any drawing activity, whether it be undertaken with pencil, paint or florist wire. To judge when an activity meets design and technology or art requirements, can be a frustrating and sterile activity. Crudely stated, you can often judge by evaluating whether the outcome is essentially functional (D&T), or aesthetic (art). Specific design activities that should be introduced into the Key Stage 2 art scheme include packaging, ceramics, designing games and fabric and textile design.

Designing requires the development of the same skills as drawing or painting. Thus, when working, the children will need to consider carefully their use of the visual elements. To concentrate on the visual elements will help the children to see that good design often, but not always, reduces images to their most basic form.

In deciding what constitutes 'good design', the children also need to be given the opportunity to study a wide range of designs. Looking at the work of a famous children's book illustrator, ceramic or fabric designers can be equally as rewarding as looking at Constable, Monet or El Greco.

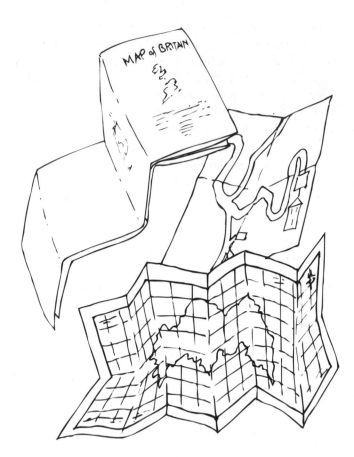

MAPPING OUT A DESIGN

To develop the ability to communicate information using signs and symbols.

†† *Whole class.*

🕐 *Three 60-minute sessions.*

Previous skills/knowledge needed
Children will need to have completed some form of mapping activities.

Key background information
This activity specifically addresses the requirement for children to use pattern in their designing, and to show how both space and shape are presented in images. It also offers the opportunity to introduce art into geography work.

Preparation
The activity requires the children to look at maps. You will need, therefore, to have some large scale maps, preferably of the local area, to show them. It will also be helpful if some hand-drawn maps of the countryside or town walks are available. Ensure that you have a contingency plan for those who live either very close to the school or a long distance away as both of these groups would find this activity of drawing a map of their journey to school very difficult.

Make enough copies of photocopiable page 137 for one between two children, if required.

Resources needed
A range of maps, pencils, paper, coloured pencils and/or paint. If required: photocopiable page 137.

What to do
Look at some of the maps with the children, concentrating on the various symbols used by map makers. Contrast the style of an Ordnance Survey map with a hand-drawn map indicating a directional walk. Discuss with them also the traditional 'Treasure Island-type' map. If you feel the children need further support, hand out photocopiable page 137 and go through it with them. Could they display their maps in a more interesting style than in the illustration? Ask them to close their eyes and consider their journey to school each day. What are the main features? Do they pass shops, a park, a copse or row of trees, a relative's house or a factory? How would they draw these features on their map if they were not allowed to use any lettering? Ask them to experiment with designing a map and then show a friend on their table to see if they recognise the location. Once the children have begun to develop some useful symbols and designs they should undertake a more detailed plan of their journey to school. To make the task easier do not stress the need for accurate proportions, rather suggest that the map should be interesting and stretch from one side of the paper to the other. They can also make the features which they wish to stand out prominently of a larger size than other, less interesting, features. Crucially, the drawing should be appealing and make stimulating reading!

Once completed the map can be coloured. It is not necessary to colour the whole map, but instead, colour along the route and include the key features. In this instance coloured pencils are appropriate. The map can now be carefully folded in the way of many maps (see illustration above), and a cover added. The cover might include some lettering and a drawing of a scene or scenes taken from the journey. Any symbols used can be added as a key on the back.

Suggestion(s) for extension
The personalising of the map can be extended by asking the children to include drawings of interesting people they meet on their journey. Thus, mum or dad may be depicted saying goodbye, and the bus driver, taxi driver, traffic supervisor or postman included. These might not be shown in exactly the position on the map that they are found on the journey but used, perhaps, as a border around the edge. Gardens could also be included.

Suggestion(s) for support
Make sure the children understand that, as well as making a map, they are involved in making a work of art. They need to remember to fill their maps with interesting detail and ensure their shapes fit together to make a pattern which will be

interesting to the observer. Hand out photocopiable page 137 to help them understand the task. Similarly, when designing the cover, encourage the children to try writing over the top of their illustrations rather than lettering at the top of the page with the picture underneath.

Assessment opportunities

Discuss the results with the children once they have completed all the tasks. Invite other children to look at the maps and see whether, from the information provided, they can recognise the author of the map. Where children show a specific aptitude for this type of design work or make a special effort, you may decide to add to your individual notes on them.

Opportunities for IT

The children could use an art or drawing package to draw their map of the route to school. They will need to be able to draw lines and change their colours and thicknesses, draw other shapes for parks or interesting buildings, fill them with colour and design other symbols for the route.

Once the map has been drawn it could be used within a word-processed guide to the journey to school. The map could be placed in the centre of the screen and text added around the outside. This is most easily done in a desktop publishing package or a word processor, which allows text to be placed into frames which can then be positioned on the page. Some packages allow lines to be

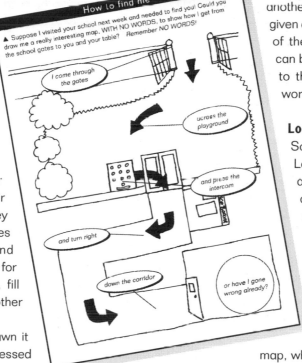

How to find me

▲ Suppose I visited your school next week and needed to find you! Could you draw me a really interesting map, WITH NO WORDS, to show how I get from the school gates to you and your table? Remember NO WORDS!

I come through the gates

across the playground

and press the intercom

and turn right

down the corridor

or have I gone wrong already?

drawn to link the frames to the places on the map. Where schools have talking word processors they could add speech to the on-screen version of the map.

An alternative approach would be to use the map as the basis for a multi-media presentation about the route to school, created using an authoring package. The children could use their computer-drawn map, or a scanned version of their hand-drawn map. Different parts of the map could be made 'live' so that when the user clicks on it, either they are taken to another screen with more information, or are given a spoken commentary about that part of the journey. The spoken commentary can be made with a microphone attached to the computer so that the children's words can be saved as a computer file.

Looking at works of art

Some of David Hockney's paintings of Los Angeles show parts of journeys and these are worth sharing with the children. A collection of good maps of walks are, however, more appropriate in this instance.

Display ideas

Rather than displaying their work on the wall, consider making a book of their maps. This could include an introduction to each map, where the child describes the journey, picking out the 'highlights' of it as shown on the map.

Reference to photocopiable sheet

Photocopiable page 137 supports the main activity. Use it either to introduce the activity if this a totally new idea for the children, or as a support for those who need it.

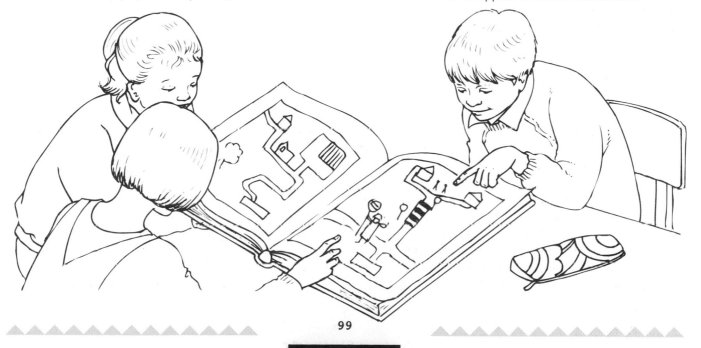

GYMNASTIC SHAPES

To understand the importance of shape in composing designs. To develop the ability to produce abstract work through expressive drawing.

†† *Two groups of up to six children.*

🕐 *Three 60-minute sessions.*

Previous skills/knowledge needed

This activity builds on work begun at Key Stage 1 where the children should have acquired a notion of positive and negative space. The children will be required to produce some quick figure drawings to a specified size.

Key background information

One of your key tasks in art lessons is to help the children understand that there is more than one way of representing the world. By the end of the key stage, many children come to the conclusion that they cannot draw and have become disillusioned by their efforts. To offset this, it is important to provide them with opportunities to undertake design work, including three-dimensional activities and a wide range of craft work. By showing them the many ways in which ideas can be expressed in a visual form, we help them to develop a confidence with their art work which is sadly lacking in most teachers!

The concept of positive and negative space is an important one and, as we have already discovered in the still-life section, well worth repeating at Key Stage 2. Simply stated, it requires the children to understand that not only is the positive shape, in this case the figure, important but also the space which surrounds it. Thus, if the children produce a drawing of a person that is very interesting but extremely small, then it will be swamped by the surrounding space. (In which case your role is very often to trim the drawing down to a size where the figure is in better proportion to the space!)

This ability to make an interesting negative space is one of the reasons why Cézanne's *Still Life with Milk Jug and Fruit* is so interesting. (If you have not undertaken the task 'Fruit, Jugs and Cézanne' on page 52, it is worth spending just a few minutes reading its 'Preparation' section.) For this activity, the design is in the organisation of shape and the arrangement of colour.

Preparation

As with a number of the activities described, the children need to begin by undertaking some quick figure drawings of classmates posing in dance positions. Ensure, therefore, that the children will be able to see the poses, and if this is not possible within the classroom then arrange to do the drawings in the hall or other large space. Organise the session so that there are two groups of up to six children doing the activity. Involve the rest of the class in another activity. One group will be the 'drawing' group, while the

other one provides the poses. You will need to provide at least six sheets of paper of varying sizes ranging from 18cm × 12cm to 6cm × 4cm. An alternative is to provide paper of the same size and then change the size of their drawings by photocopying. This is, however, a very expensive method.

Make sufficient copies of photocopiable page 138 so that there is one between two children.

Resources needed

Paper as described in 'Preparation' section above, sketching or 2B pencils, rubbers, scissors, large paper for the final composition, paints, brushes, water pots, rags, newspaper, photocopiable page 138. For extension activity: clay.

What to do

Introduce the task by handing out photocopiable page 138 and asking all the children to draw five gymnastic figures in different positions on a rectangular piece of paper. This should not take them long as the idea is to look at the shapes made, not to do perfect figure drawing. Ask them to join the ends of the paper and think of how they could use it as a functional object. For example, they might suggest a lampshade or a design for a mug. Let them cut up their sheet and rearrange the figures on another sheet. How could they make them really colourful? Tell them to join the two ends again. What could they use this for? Perhaps they could glue the design on to a cardboard box to make a pencil case. (See photocopiable page 134 for a pencil box-making exercise.) Once this activity is over, move on to the main task.

Explain to the drawing group that they are to produce six, five-minute drawings. They should begin on the smallest piece of paper and work through the drawings to the largest. On each drawing, however, they must make sure that their drawing fills the paper, fitting to all edges. If this does not appear possible because of the arrangement of the pose,

then the children will need to exaggerate the length of the arms, for example, to make sure they do adhere to the rules! They need not worry about the detail of the clothing and can, if they wish, do the drawing as a silhouette. Their concern should be with the shape of the figure and the shapes of the spaces in the corners of the drawing. Ask the group of children posing to adopt interesting dance poses. To make the poses easier to 'hold' you may suggest they lean against a wall so that they can stand with an arm above their head or with legs bent. Give the children as many rests as they need. The groups can now swap roles, with the drawing group posing.

At the end of the session all the children should have at least six silhouette drawings of various sizes. They should cut these out and use them as templates to draw round. Working on the large piece of paper they can now make an arrangement, repeating figures where necessary and working with the figures in all directions, some upside down and others horizontal. You may consider asking one group to overlap their drawings and the other group to place their figures separately.

Remind them of the need to make an interesting arrangement and ask them to look specifically at the shapes they are making between the figures.

When finished, ask the children to consider whether their designs would be improved by the addition of head-dresses or swirling skirts. They should then paint their completed designs in bright, flat colours.

Suggestion(s) for extension

There are many ways of extending this work. Ask the children to select one section of their picture that they particularly like and repeat it to form a stamp design. They should select an area where the figure or figures are cut off rather than choosing a central pose. In a similar manner, they can produce a clay panel.

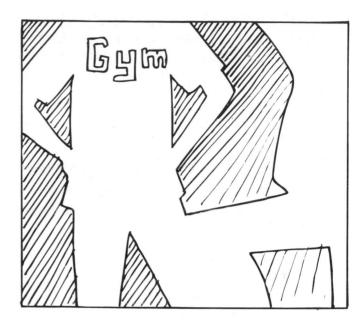

A more difficult, but very interesting, task is to use their finished design as a record sleeve (or CD inlay card, but this is restrictive in space). When completed they can decide on a short title and consider how best they can incorporate the lettering into their designs.

Suggestion(s) for support

Once the children have understood the task or tasks they should be able to continue with limited support. During the initial drawing session, however, much encouragement and advice is necessary. At the end of each pose, select one or two examples which you feel demonstrate the essence of the task. An example would be where the child, through exaggerating the pose, has managed to work to all edges, creating a dynamic set of shapes.

Assessment opportunities

Note those children who are able to follow the instructions and interpret them in an exciting way. Add relevant comments to your individual notes. At the end of all the work, discuss and evaluate it with the children. Ask questions: 'Who can remember what we had to do when we did the quick drawings? Does this picture where all the arms and legs have been lengthened look better than others? Why is this? Do the spiky head-dresses make the designs look more interesting? Do the colours used go well with the shapes? Are the background shapes in this particular work more interesting than the dancers themselves?'

Opportunities for IT

Some children could extend this work using a drawing package. They could draw their silhouettes, either all on the same 'computer page', or allow a different screen for each drawing; saving them to disk each time. These could be printed out and used as templates to complete the larger design work.

Alternatively the children could make the final design on the screen. They need to reduce the size of their silhouettes to fit the much smaller paper available. To do this they will need to be able to group all of the parts of a silhouette together to make a single object, which can then be scaled, rotated, copied or flipped and moved into position to make the design.

Looking at works of art

The theme for this activity is based very much on Benin art. By working with figures of different sizes the children will have produced hierarchical drawings (although they will not realise this unless you tell them!), and by working with their dancers placed in varying directions, they will have worked even more closely to the style of some Benin artists. It is not, however, vital that the children are shown Benin art for this activity to be successful.

Matisse painted a picture of dancers that is simple in form and is a great example of the importance of positive and negative space. This picture, called *The Dance,* is much reproduced and you should have little difficulty finding a copy.

Display ideas

If possible take photographs of the children in the original poses so that other children in the school can see the starting point for the work.

Reference to photocopiable sheet

Photocopiable page 138 allows the children to adapt quickly drawn design arrangements as the basis for functional objects. The sheet is used as an introduction to the main activity.

CIRCULAR SECTIONS

To develop understanding of the functional aspects of design.

†† *Whole class or small groups.*

⏱ *Three 60-minute sessions.*

Previous skills/knowledge needed

This activity develops issues raised in 'Gymnastic shapes' on page 100. It is helpful but not vital that the children have undertaken this earlier activity.

Key background information

While much of the designing that the children will undertake is theoretical, it is very beneficial if, from time to time, they are given the opportunity to work on a practical activity. Try to ensure that the children are given a good-sized paper plate on to which they can add their final design. By undertaking drawings of specific parts of the bicycle and not the whole, you are encouraging the children to make informed selections. The ability to select from a wide range of information needs steadily developing throughout this and subsequent key stages.

This activity requires the children to trace some of their drawings. At times tracing is an acceptable activity, particularly where the children are involved in a designing task. Many graphic designers extract images from photographs, scan on to computer images and then make alterations as required. In these instances it is the final idea that is the key outcome, not the process involved.

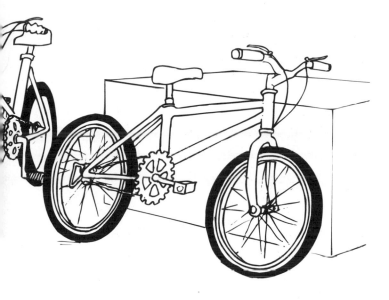

By giving them quite small pieces of paper (A5) you need to ensure that the children work to full size, filling the paper and not worrying too much if the drawing is not centrally arranged. (It is better if it is not.)

When the drawings are complete, the children should trace all three drawings and arrange the tracings on to the larger paper. In this case it does not matter if they do not work to the edges but they should look to create interesting shapes within shapes. This completed, they can now take the plate and, overlaying it on top of their design, select the most interesting section and draw around the edge of the plate. This will enable them to see how their final design will look. If, on reflection, they consider they have not made the best choice, further circles can be added. The children's final designs can either be traced on to the plates and painted, or the shapes can be traced on to coloured paper and stuck on to the plate to create a collage design. If painting on the plate is difficult because of a wax coating, then the final design can be traced on to paper, painted, and then, as a whole, cut out and stuck on to the plate.

For a further session, as with the above activity, the children can begin by designing from the shapes they see but this time from looking at the workings of a clock. They can then use their design in a functional manner. Hand out photocopiable page 139. Explain to the children that the composition should appear stronger working in black and white rather than using colour. If some children finish the task quickly, ask them to do the same activity, but using colour to compare results.

Preparation

Arrange the room or space so that all the children involved are able to see the bicycle. Make sure that all the appropriate resources are available. You may wish to read through the notes and sketch out some of the possibilities so as to be aware of the potential the activity offers.

Find some 'wind up' clocks, boxes the size of watches, and make enough copies of photocopiable page 139 for one copy between every three to five children, if required.

Resources needed

At least one, and if the whole class is involved at the same time, possibly more, bicycles, three or more sheets of sketching paper (A5), large sheets of paper, pencils, rubbers, tracing paper, paints or coloured paper, adhesive, medium or large paper plates (one per child), Poster of Clarice Cliff's work *Bizarre* (poster in separately available pack accompanying this book or your own version). If required: photocopiable page 139, boxes and 'wind up' clocks.

What to do

Begin by discussing the Clarice Cliff designs with the children. Discuss the characteristics of the designs, in particular noting how the final design is a simplification of the original view or object. The shapes used are strong and bold but quite simple. The designer has not drawn in every detail but has used only the most important lines and shapes.

When drawing the bicycles, the children should select only small sections and not try to draw the whole. Point out that, once they have completed their drawings, they will be required to assemble several of them together, to create an interesting design with which to decorate a plate. When drawing, therefore, they should concentrate on all the circular sections – the cogs, wheels, spokes, chain – and perhaps the brake and gear cables.

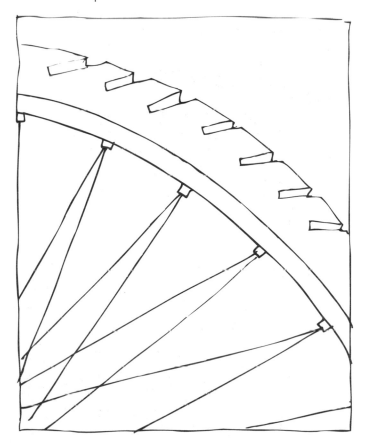

Suggestion(s) for extension

This activity can be extended by asking the children to take another, second, rectangular section of their design which can be transferred in the same way on to a mug, for example.

Suggestion(s) for support

At each stage of the task be prepared to intervene and ask questions of the children. Do they consider the section they have drawn to be interesting? Are the shapes they are producing large, bold and clear? When overlapping are they creating new, interesting shapes? Should they leave out some of the lines so that the outside space can 'break into' the positive shapes? By questioning, you help the children to focus on the most important aspects of the activity.

A time design

Clocks are fascinating

or at least the old-fashioned ones!

▲ Make some studies of parts of a 'wind up' clock.
▲ Cover an old box with black or white paper.
▲ Cut out some strong simple clock shapes based on your sketches (again using black or white paper) and stick them on to your box.

Would people buy a clock in the interesting box you have designed?

Assessment opportunities

Discuss the final outcomes with the children. Ask them to make a comparison between their designs and those of Clarice Cliff. Does their work share the same characteristics? Add to your individual notes on children where they show a particular aptitude for this type of design work.

Opportunities for IT

This work could be extended by using a computer drawing package. The children could either redraw their sketches using the software, or draw directly from the bicycles. Alternatively, they could scan in their line drawings to make a computer image. If a digital camera is available, children could work from a complete picture of the bicycle, using the various tools to cut out the parts of the bike they want to use – children with less-developed drawing skills could use this approach.

Once the children have the pictures on the computer screen, they can experiment by moving them around the screen to create their design. They can copy, rotate or flip the shapes and once they have arranged them, they can use the circle drawing tool to mask the area they have chosen for the plate. In order to be able to see through the circle the children need to select a 'no fill' or transparent fill option for the circle. The whole screen picture can then be printed out, the circular part cut out and stuck on to the paper plate. The same technique could be used for the rectangular design for a mug.

Looking at works of art

The Clarice Cliff poster is used as a stimulus in this activity.

Display ideas

Pin a plain tablecloth flat to the display board and fix the children's plate designs to it.

Reference to photocopiable sheet

Photocopiable page 139 provides a further activity where the final idea is the key outcome. This time the children design the pattern for a watch box by using the shapes of the workings of a 'wind up' clock.

JEWELS OF THE SEA

To design and make functional items. To work as a member of a team.

†† *Whole class in groups of eight.*

🕒 *Three 60-minute sessions.*

Previous skills/knowledge needed

This activity builds on the previous activities in this chapter.

Key background information

Many activities require children to work from a specific brief. This allows the children to learn important technical and design skills and to experiment within tight constraints. It is also necessary, however, to allow the children opportunities to make a wider range of decisions for themselves and to work as a member of a team. On such occasions, the range of materials made available is critical as this forms the method of constraining choice.

Design

Preparation

While this activity can be arranged in a number of ways the children may gain the most benefit if arranged in groups of eight. This will allow you to explain the task of making a range of jewellery based on the theme of the sea. The children should then decide how, as a group, they will undertake the various parts of the task. Before beginning, ensure that an appropriate range of materials is available from which the group can choose.

Make enough copies of photocopiable page 140 for two between each group, if required.

Resources needed

Stimulus materials (for example books on the sea and sea-life, shells and pebbles, interesting pieces of jewellery), clay, 'Fimo' or Plasticine, card and shiny papers, newspaper, pieces of material and lace, sequins, florist wire, adhesive, paint, brushes, kitchen foil. This list may be added to following initial discussions with the group. If required: photocopiable page 140. For extension activity: small cardboard boxes.

What to do

Start by showing the children one or two interesting pieces of jewellery. Discuss the function of jewellery with them and brainstorm a list of the different forms that jewellery can take. Organise the class into groups of eight (it may be best to ensure they include both boys and girls).

Explain the task to the children. The groups should see themselves as rival design studios. Their task is to bring out a new range of jewellery based on the theme of the sea. They should produce at least five separate pieces, for example: brooch, badge, bracelet, earrings, necklace, bangle and so on. They should include a wide range of materials in the designs.

Before beginning remind all groups of the characteristics of good design (for example simplicity, form and shape). Discuss how a bracelet might be made, for example by twisting a coil of paper, taping the ends then covering with material or netting; or how they might use card to make a brooch and then cover with shiny papers. You may also suggest that they have a unifying theme to their work, all working from fish or shells and pebbles, or deciding on a very limited range of colours.

The children should look for source material from which to work and undertake some design drawings before beginning to make their items. They also need to decide how they are going to work. Five pieces of jewellery and eight children means they will need to make decisions concerning the division of labour! While they are making decisions and undertaking their designs, discuss the range of materials each group requires and check they are clear as to how they will undertake the task. It is as well to set a time limit, allowing them no more than two sessions to complete the task.

For a further session, hand out photocopiable page 140. Each group can make two mirrors with stiff card as the frame. Allow the children to decorate the frames in as creative a way as they see fit.

Suggestion(s) for extension

If the children have retained their enthusiasm, extend the project by asking them to make a box for storing their jewellery. They should cover it using a suitable design, make labels to attach to the jewellery and design a logo for their design studio. Finally, they should design a small section of wrapping paper to be used to wrap those items which are not boxed.

Suggestion(s) for support

Try to offer as much support as possible before the groups become too involved in the activity. It is best to cool their enthusiasm a little and make sure that they have fully understood the possibilities and the restrictions before they start. Be prepared to go through some of the processes. If, for example, they are to use clay, give all the children a brief reminder of the procedures they should follow. Perhaps suggest some ways in which it could be used to good advantage in, for example, the making of beads. You should also be clear as to whether they can use only the materials you have supplied or add others of their choice.

Assessment opportunities

At the end of the activity you may wish to call in another teacher or a few parents to help you decide on the various merits of the design studio groups' work! Look for good quality craftsmanship, design strengths and consistency

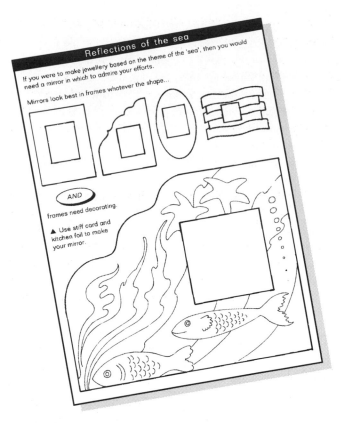

throughout the range. If this were a real exercise, which range would you decide to buy and sell in your shop?

Opportunities for IT

The children could be given access to an art or a drawing package which will enable them to show their IT capability in the design stage of the work. They could also create marketing and promotional materials for their products.

The children could use the software to create their jewellery design, the pattern for wrapping paper or a logo for their company. They could go on to use a word processor or desktop publishing package to create advertising materials, or an information catalogue for a final display.

A sophisticated approach would be to use an authoring package to create a multi-media presentation. This could include pictures drawn using an art package or scanned from children's line drawings, photographs or pictures taken using a digital camera. Moving pictures could be added using a video camera. Sound could be included in the form of voices, or even a musical background with music performed by the children and recorded using a microphone attached to the computer. The final display could be interactive so that, by clicking on a piece of jewellery, information about it was displayed, or it could be set up to be a rolling demonstration of the group's work.

Looking at works of art

At the end of the activity show them again, one or two pieces of professionally made jewellery and discuss the factors involved in making an interesting piece.

Display ideas

The groups should be asked to produce a display of their work as part of the task. When assessed, you may discuss with them how they could improve their displays so that they can be seen by the rest of the school.

Reference to photocopiable sheet

Photocopiable page 140 is an extension of the main activity. It could, however, be used as an activity in its own right, if the jewellery is not to be made. The children should explore a range of designs before starting.

IMPROVING FROM MUSIC

To develop the use of shapes and colours to express feeling. To create a spontaneous design.

†† *Whole class working individually.*

🕐 *Two or three 45- to 60-minute sessions.*

Previous skills/knowledge needed

The length of the sessions will need to take into account the ability of the children to sustain concentration over long periods of time.

Key background information

Kandinsky (a Russian painter active in Germany during the first decades of the twentieth century) entitled some of his paintings as 'Improvisations', which he said were inspired by 'inner nature'. This idea of working from the soul rather than from direct subject matter has interested artists for centuries. The work of artists such as Ernst, Miró or Klee is based on similar lines. These artists are considered to be some of the members of the Surrealism movement, which originated in France in the 1920s. This movement uses figurative elements to represent unreal, dreamlike worlds. Surrealist art is popular with many children. This is, therefore, an important activity to undertake with them and not to be seen, in any way, as a time-filler.

To create designs working expressively from imagination is an important element of national curricula requirements. To work intuitively when designing is equally as important as working systematically.

Preparation

Consider carefully the piece of music to be played. It is beneficial if, while playing different selections before the session, you attempt the task in order to get a feel for the way the children might respond to the stimulus. It may be preferable to choose something quite slow and haunting as this should encourage the children to relax, listen and slowly develop their lines, shapes and colours. If they are to listen to the music throughout the session then music which retains its basic form will help the children to work at a consistent pace. In writing this activity, *Spirit of the Rainforest* by Terry Oldfield (New World Cassettes, NWC [1990]) has been used as the stimulus. The music is haunting and incorporates two distinct sounds: tribal rhythms and noises; and music with Western wind instruments overlaid. This type of music would be ideal.

When listening and visualising the possible outcomes, decide whether the music should be interpreted chronologically or as a whole. In other words, should the children be given a long thin strip of paper so that they can work along it from left to right, or should the paper be a more traditional rectangular shape so that they can work at any point, slowly covering the whole surface?

Finally, decide whether the children are to work first in pencil, charcoal or ink before using colour, or whether they are to work directly with colour. In making this decision, you may find that when having a brief practice yourself, you discover that it is difficult to think about shape and colour simultaneously. In which case, decide to allow the children to relax, let the pencil go for a walk across the surface of the paper, and concentrate only on shape and rhythm. They can add the colour later.

While many of the activities urge the use of paint rather than pencil or pastel, in this instance in order that the children do not lose the spontaneity of the exercise, it is preferable for them to be given pastels with which to work. To aid them with their pastel work, supply them with neutral-coloured sugar or activity paper. The coarseness of the grain provides a better surface for pastels than smooth cartridge paper.

Make enough copies of photocopiable page 141 so that there is one for each child.

Resources needed

An appropriate piece of music, activity (or sugar) paper cut to the desired shape, pencils, charcoal or felt-tipped pens, pastels, photocopiable page 141. For extension activity: viewfinder.

What to do

Hand out photocopiable page 141 to each child and discuss the first point. Then complete the sheet by doing some warm-up exercises first. Ask the children to draw a series of lines representing different moods. For example, ask them to draw lines which are strong and heavy, light and thin, nervous and shaky, zigzagging, twisting, smooth, broken, slow and ponderous. Discuss their drawings with them. Remind the children that as they work on the main task they should use a similar variety of lines that correspond to the music. Give them an opportunity to explore the possibilities using pastels. Can they produce colours which represent happiness? Quietude? Fast movement? Do combinations of colours work well together?

Having discussed the results, ask them to listen to two or three minutes of the music you have chosen. This should help to get them into the right frame of mind. They should listen in silence and, at the end of the introduction, not be asked to respond but to keep their thoughts to themselves. Before beginning, explain to them that the music will last for as long as they need and that they should, therefore, work slowly and carefully.

Now start the music again and ask them to begin drawing. If they are working chronologically then they should start at one end of the paper and work their way across, otherwise they can begin at any point. Allow them to work in silence for as long as necessary. Once they have finished, if not working in colour, they should quietly pick up the pastels and start the colour work without disturbing those still drawing. There is no need to interrupt unless you sense the class or group are tiring. Be aware of children who are concerned about 'where they are' with their picture. They may feel they have done all they can, but their friends are still drawing. They may continue adding, usually unnecessary, marks to their drawing, which may detract from it.

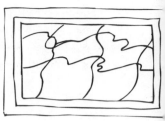

Do not attempt to complete the work in one session, but allow them a second and perhaps third, where they continue to develop the colour work with the music playing quietly in the background. Throughout, encourage them to work in silence so that they can fully concentrate on producing a unified picture.

Suggestion(s) for extension

Children finishing early should be asked to make a viewfinder and move it over their work until they isolate the area of their picture which they feel has been most successful. This can then be redrawn on to another piece of paper and lettering laid over the top. If, for example, their pictures have been inspired by listening to the *Spirit of the Rainforest*, then this may be printed over the top of their design to create a record cover (or CD inlay card, although this is restrictive in space). Alternatively, they might themselves choose a word or words which they feel sum up the mood of their work. Consider this as a task for the earliest finishers.

Suggestion(s) for support

Unless the children are failing to concentrate fully, try not to intervene. The intention of this task has been to allow the children to express personal feelings and emotions. To intervene, therefore, may not be appropriate. Be aware, however, of the point mentioned in 'What to do' where some children may continue adding to their drawing unnecessarily.

Assessment opportunities

When children work on tasks of this nature, assessment may not be appropriate beyond noting those children who respond well to this form of stimulus and who are able to sustain concentration throughout the sessions.

Opportunities for IT

Some children might like to use an art package to create a computer copy of a part of their picture which they think works well. They could add their final computer picture to a word-processed file and make a title for their work of art.

If the school has access to a colour scanner, children could scan in parts of their final pictures or photographs of their work, or use a digital camera to create images that can be used on the computer. These pictures could be used within an authoring package to create a multi-media 'slide show' of their pictures. The inspirational music can be played as a background to the show.

A picture fit for playing

▲ Imagine painting a picture for a musician to play! Which musical instrument would be needed to play this drawing?

or this?

or even this?

▲ Can you design a picture using shapes, lines and colour for a musician to interpret? Practise some ideas to start with.

Looking at works of art

Kandinsky has been referred to at the beginning of these notes. His work is well worth looking at with the children at the end of this activity. They may find they have some understanding of what he was attempting. His work is very accessible. Try to find one of his 'Improvisations' rather than his later 'Compositions'. Discuss the various shapes and lines and look carefully at his choice of colours. If he had been listening to music when working, what sort of music do they think it was? (Kandinsky was a good friend of Schoenberg, this may be worth knowing!) The work of Ernst, Klee and Miró are also relevant considerations.

Display ideas

If the children have been working chronologically, consider pinning their pictures end to end to form a long continuous strip. Otherwise, show them individually with an appropriate frame for each. As the work has been very personal, ask the children to choose for themselves the colour of the backing paper which best suits their work.

Reference to photocopiable sheet

Photocopiable page 141 can be used as a stimulus for and an introduction to the main activity. Discuss the illustrations with the children before asking them to try out one or two ideas themselves. Once they have become accustomed to this idea, they can then begin to create and colour their pictures for interpretation into music.

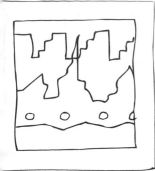

 AMAZING BOARD GAME

To develop understanding of the roles that colour, shape and texture play in creating patterns.

†† *Whole class working in pairs.*

🕐 *Three 60-minute sessions.*

Key background information

The National Curriculum requires children to use and experience texture and pattern in designing and making. This activity fulfils this requirement as well as showing how colour is applied in images and design.

Preparation

While this activity can be undertaken perfectly well without reference to the work of other artists, it would enhance the children's work if you were able to show them an example of the work of Michael Brennand-Wood. (His work was featured in *Art & Craft* magazine, published by Scholastic, in January 1997.)

Ensure that there are sufficient resources available for all those participating.

Resources needed

Stiff cardboard, approximately 40cm × 30cm, paints, a wide range of papers, scraps of materials, ribbons, adhesive, paintbrushes, sewing tools and other materials which may be appropriate.

What to do

If you have been able to find an example of Brennand-Wood's textile and mixed media work then discuss this with the children. Note how he uses his materials, building up layers and adding to the subtlety of the composition by changing the colours or the configurations as he works. If his work is not available, then begin by introducing the children to the activity.

Working in pairs, ask the children to design a board game. They should draw their designs on to card. Explain that the game does not have to be played. Their task is to make it look like a board game – it should tease so that people will look at it and wonder how it works! (Rather like a board game that is dug up after thousands of years, with no instructions, and only the design of the board being available.)

Their game should consist of squares, circles or tessellating shapes. Some shapes should be given a specific colour which is then reproduced in varying densities at another point on the board. The observer will think that they should follow these coloured shapes in order to discover their importance. The children could include some arrows or lines which indicate a certain direction the 'player' should follow. It is not necessary to add any lettering.

Once pairs have completed their design sketches, they can be transferred to the board. When they add colour, rather than painting flat colours, ask them to work with collage materials. Thus, they may incorporate some bright, shiny squares or tissue-paper circles. The aim should be to confuse observers, to make them look across the surface of the board in an attempt to work out how the pattern is arranged, thereby coming to an understanding of the significance of the pattern.

Suggestion(s) for extension

Once the main task is completed, the children, still working in their pairs, may wish to make some counters to add to the board. Again, these should be large, simple designs, not over fussy, so that they hint at some connection with their game. One or two of the pairs may enjoy tantalising the

onlooker further by writing one or two rules. They may, for example, point out that one should follow the red squares in order of colour density before trying to 'capture' those on the blue circles. Alternatively, a box may be made to store some counters.

Suggestions for support

Be prepared to offer considerable help at the planning stage, ensuring that they work with interesting patterns and do not attempt to over-complicate the task. Consider the range of materials that they will need to complete their collage and ask them whether their work will be better if they find some of the materials for themselves.

Assessment opportunities

At the completion of the work, discuss the results with the pairs. What is it about some board games that make them more interesting than others? Where pairs have used a limited range of shapes and colours, have they been successful in creating an interesting pattern? Which pairs have achieved the best craftsmanship? Encourage the children to evaluate for themselves, thereby increasing their learning and understanding.

Opportunities for IT

The children could use a drawing or art package to help them with the design of their game. They could also use a word processor to draft some rules for the game.

A more ambitious project would be to use an authoring package to create an interactive multi-media game. A selection of starting shapes could be shown on the first screen and, when children click on one, they are taken to a screen showing a number of other shapes. Children can then select another shape and move to the next screen. In this way the children only ever see a small sample of the playing board, if indeed there is one! The screens could be accompanied by music or other sound effects or pictures. Children could use their imagination in creating the most interesting screens full of patterns and shapes. As this is an imaginary game there is no need to have an end position or any real focus to the game!

Looking at works of art

The work of Michael Brennand-Wood has already been referred to in 'Preparation' above. It is also worth showing the children examples of Aboriginal art, as it consistently includes patterns which need to be 'read'. Show the children this work at the end rather than at the beginning of the activity, otherwise there will be a tendency to create 'dotty' patterns, which is not the requirement in this instance.

Display ideas

Display their work, with the children adding a question or two to make the observer stop and look carefully. Their boards may be scored and slightly folded to increase the appearance of a board game.

Photocopiables

The pages in this section can be photocopied for use in the classroom or school which has purchased this book, and do not need to be declared in any return in respect of any photocopying licence.

They comprise a varied selection of both pupil and teacher resources, including pupil worksheets, resource material and record sheets to be completed by the teacher or children. Most of the photocopiable sheets are related to individual activities in the book; the name of the activity is indicated at the top of the sheet, together with a page reference indicating where the lesson plan for that activity can be found.

Individual pages are discussed in detail within each lesson plan, accompanied by ideas for adaptation where appropriate – of course, each sheet can be adapted to suit your own needs and those of your class. Sheets can also be coloured, laminated, mounted on to card, enlarged and so on where appropriate.

Pupil worksheets and record sheets have spaces provided for children's names and for noting the date on which each sheet was used. This means that, if so required, they can be included easily within any pupil assessment portfolio.

Investigating the classroom, see page 17 and Reflecting on line and tone, see page 60

Reflections of me

Drawing yourself in
the mirror is easy!

But can you
draw your
reflection in
a kettle?

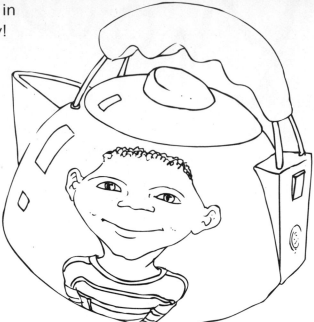

or a Christmas bauble?

or the hub-cap of a car?

*How many things can you
find where you can see and
draw your reflection?*

ART

Investigating the classroom, see page 17

Reflecting on objects

We can draw an interesting still life.

(BUT) What happens if we add a mirror?

(AND THEN) We use a viewfinder and draw only part of the still life and part of the reflection? Can you draw that?

Changing world, see page 20

My 'orange' sketchbook

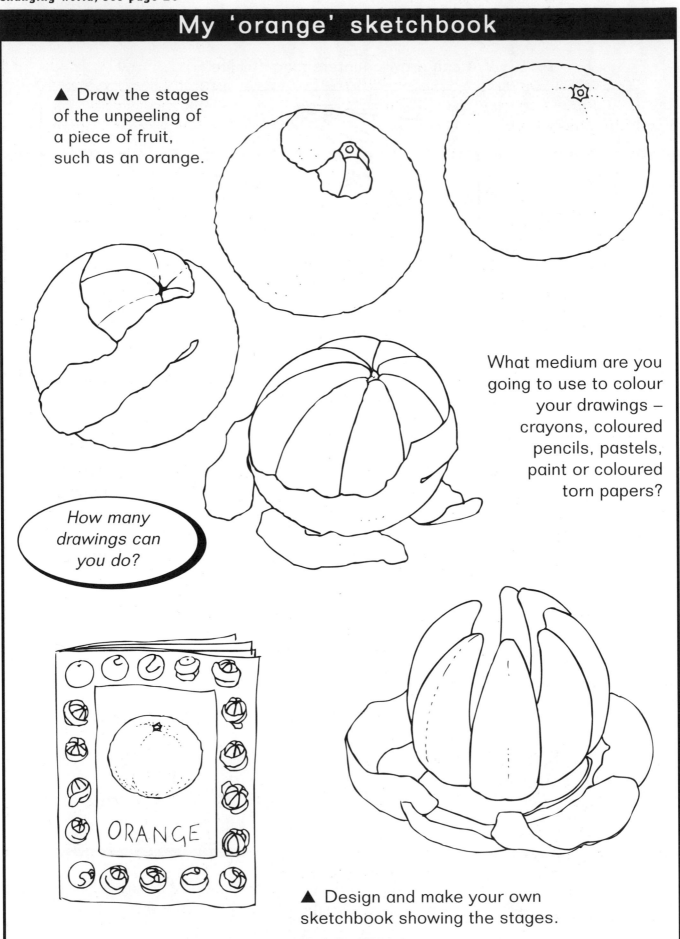

▲ Draw the stages of the unpeeling of a piece of fruit, such as an orange.

What medium are you going to use to colour your drawings – crayons, coloured pencils, pastels, paint or coloured torn papers?

How many drawings can you do?

ORANGE

▲ Design and make your own sketchbook showing the stages.

ART

Investigating paper textures, see page 22

My book of textures

... drawing an apple with oil pastels on very smooth glasspaper.

Just imagine...

Or drawing the apple with chalk and charcoal on brown wrapping paper.

You could paint it on to a kitchen paper towel...

... or use felt-tipped pens on coloured tissue paper.

You could even draw the apple with torn strips of newspaper.

Then you would have a book of apple textures.

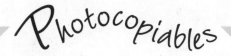

Sketching from unusual angles, see page 25

Interesting angles

Sometimes my drawings look more interesting
if I sit on the floor!

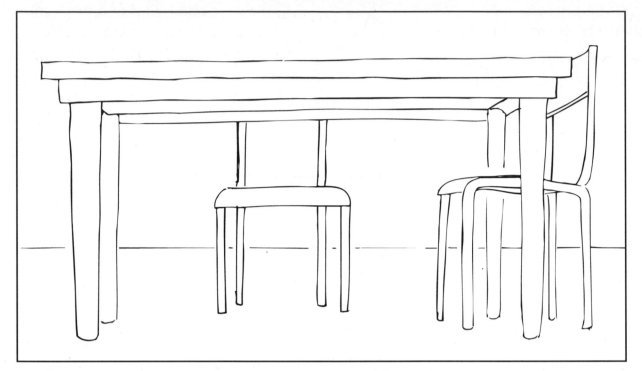

OR   close up to a plant.

OR   I look down on a still life.

Where can you stand or sit to make interesting drawings?

Speeding into figure drawing, see page 30

My five-minute book

Imagine a book where each of the drawings were done in no more than 5 minutes!

Use a stopwatch to make sure you don't cheat!

Drawings of my classroom

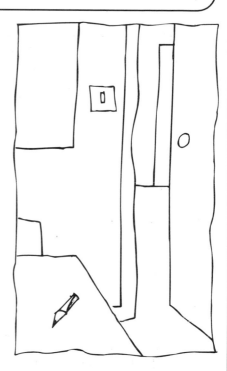

OR Drawings of the people on our table

Can you draw them in colour?

It's amazing how much you can draw in five minutes!

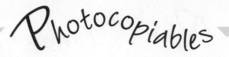
A fresh view of the family, see page 34

My family

Before the camera was invented many rich families had their family portrait painted.

▲ Imagine you were to paint a picture of your family. Can you organise them into an interesting arrangement showing how important they all are, or, perhaps so they look pleasing to the eye?

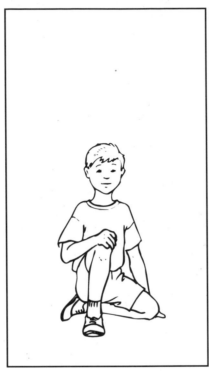

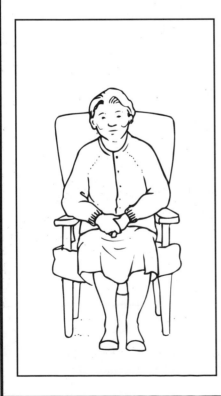

Me and my favourite things, see page 37

This is me

If you were to send a 'map' of yourself to people in outer space would it look like this?

Hugo aged 10

Me in my Arsenal kit

▲ How would you arrange your map? What things would you add to explain what you were like?

Exploring the visual elements, see page 38

Textured portraits

Sometimes our drawings look more interesting if we add texture.

1   Draw a picture of the person sitting opposite you.

2   Roll out a LITTLE printing ink on to a flat board.

3   Lay your drawing on top.

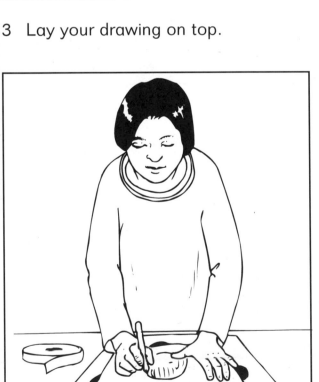

4   Turn the paper over and you have a very interesting textured drawing.

▲ Now experiment by pressing with your finger or adding more than one colour.

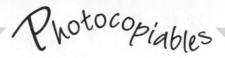
Looking at emotions, see page 41

Colour charting the way I feel!

What colour is happiness?

What colour would you be if you were jealous?

What colour makes you sad?

What colour would you be if you were lonely?

Can you mix a colour to describe being ill?

Can you make a colour chart for emotions?

Happiness is red and blue because

_____

Loneliness is _____ because

_____

Which colours will you now choose to paint your portrait? When you have finished can your friends guess your emotion?

ART

My friend's face, see page 46

My friend's face

Just imagine you were a tiny spider
and you dropped onto the end of your friend's nose!

▲ Look *carefully* at your friend's nose. Can you draw the path of the little spider as it explores your friend's face? Keep looking and never take your pencil off the paper as you follow the spider's travels.

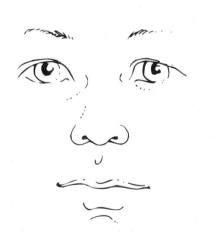

▲ Now try a colour picture of your friend using pastels. Again start at the tip of the nose and work outwards. Don't worry about the edge but really concentrate on the area around the nose.

REMEMBER!
KEEP LOOKING

An angle on shoes, see page 55

Nine angles on my shoe

Shoes are very interesting to draw especially if you draw them large and bold with chalk and charcoal.

▲ Can you make nine interesting pictures of your shoe?

How will you make each picture different?

Colour?   Print?   Collage?   Texture?   Magnify?   Upside-down?

ART

Colour in a corner, see page 57

A flashy still life

▲ Arrange a group of objects in the corner of your classroom.
Remember to choose things with simple bold shapes.
▲ Can you use your collection of papers to make a big bold flashy collage?

A plant, bowl of fruit and some cloth

▲ Make a collection of the brightest-coloured papers you can find.

Gummed paper

Coloured tin foil

Sweet wrappers

Gift wrapping paper

Glossy magazines

A fresh look at flowers, see page 62

A close up on colour

▲ Choose a flower which is in full bloom.
▲ Make a small viewfinder which, when held close to the flower, allows you to see only part of the flower.
▲ Make three or four small, quick colour sketches.
Which one has the most interesting shapes?

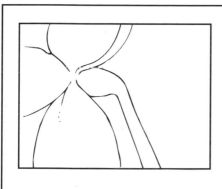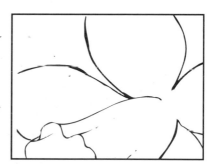

▲ Can you now do a very large painting of your favourite sketch?

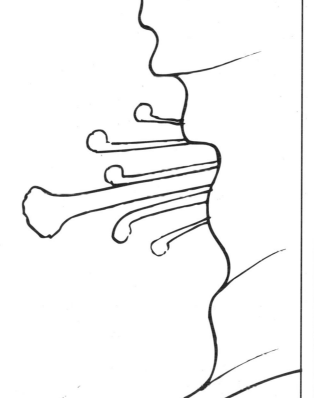

You will need to mix lots of subtly changing colours if your picture is to look really interesting.

Guitars, violins and trumpets for art, see page 64

A fresh look at shape

  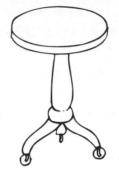 

▲ Choose four interesting objects to draw – but don't draw them yet!
▲ Cut eight rectangles of different sizes.

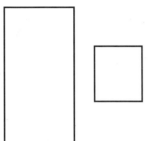 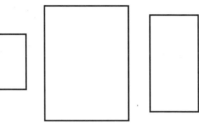  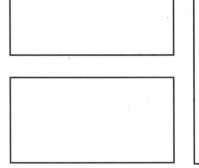

▲ Now draw parts of the objects on to each rectangle.

▲ Overlap the rectangles on a piece of paper and stick them down.

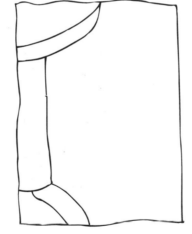

You may like to paint or collage your drawing and add further parts of the objects, but remember to:

KEEP LOOKING FOR INTERESTING SHAPES!

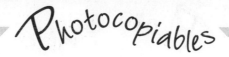

A famous painting comes to life

▲ Begin by choosing an interesting landscape.
(*Toledo* by El Greco would be a good example but there are many more you could work from.)

Toledo foreground

▲ Make some sketches in which you try to analyse the shapes of the foreground, middle ground and background.

Toledo middle ground

Toledo background

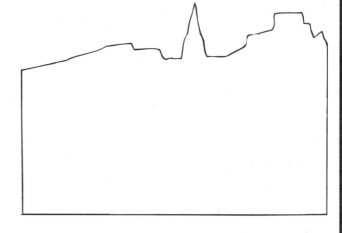

▲ Roll out a slab of clay and cut out the fore-, middle and background, and 'stick' onto a base slab.
   You may decide you then want to add some joining slabs to give a more detailed 3D appearance to your work.

Landscape through a window, see page 71

Do you see what I see?

▲ Work with a small group of friends (five or six would be ideal). Arrange yourselves, sitting close together in front of a window.
▲ Either choose a window pane each or stick squares of masking tape on to the window so you each have your own view.
▲ Keep very still and draw the view through your window frame. Each one of you will become a camera taking a snapshot of the view.
▲ Now display your drawings to show how the view alters quite significantly from only a small change in viewpoint.

Tackling landscape, see page 73

Walking into a weaving

▲ Imagine going for a walk along a river's edge, tripping through long grass, battling with brambles and gliding through bluebells.
Could you describe your walk through a weaving?
It might look something like this:

Bluebells
Lilac, blue and green materials

Brambles
Greens and browns, perhaps some brambles stuck in

Grasses
Long thin grasses

River
Blue ribbons

▲ Perhaps you could go for a walk and collect some materials on the way to use in your weaving, rather than working from memory.

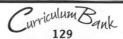

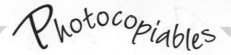

Visiting the church, see page 78

Inside/outside

Instead of making just one drawing of a building many artists have put two or three drawings together. In this sketch you can see the outside shape of the church, part of the inside, and part of the churchyard – three drawings in one to make an interesting assemblage of this church.

▲ Do several drawings of your school to include a silhouette of the shape, drawings of the inside and the playground or playing field. Now see if you can put them together in an interesting way.

The modern landscape, see page 80

Sketching signs and symbols

▲ As you drive, cycle or walk to school every day how many different signs do you see? Can you draw them all? When you go home tonight check to see how many you missed and to see if you made any mistakes.

▲ Use your sketches to make a landscape of shapes from all the various signs. You may like to overlap your signs and make them look transparent. You may also wish to add cars, people on bikes and parts of buildings.
There are many ways you may wish to draw, paint or print a picture of the landscape you pass as you go to school.

Starting to sail, see page 84

Wrapping up

▲ Experiment with sheets of tissue paper painted with a thin layer of a mixture of PVA glue and water. Begin by wrapping the paper around a balsa or wire frame you have made to make the frame solid.

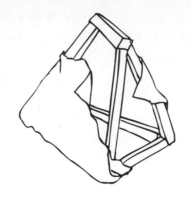

▲ Frames are not the only things you can wrap. Try doing the same thing with these objects.

Wrap them carefully so the tissue doesn't tear.

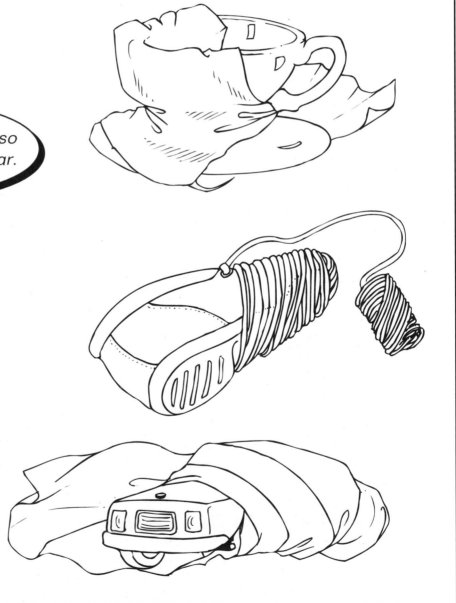

▲ Try wrapping a similar object using plain cloth and wool and string. Make sure you can still see what it is when you have finished!

▲ What other materials can you use to wrap these objects to make very interesting shapes?

ART

Developing the clay scene, see page 86

The town on the hill

1 Roll out a slab of clay and lay it over an upturned saucer.
Do not cut off the overlapping pieces.

2 Now make some small blocks to be your houses, factories and churches. Using a small modelling tool, press in the windows and doors and add a roof.

3 Make small balls of clay. Press a small amount of clay through a sieve and add this on to three balls to make bushes and trees.

4 Begin to construct your 'town'. Press in the paths and use small pieces of bark to press on to the base to make the textures of fields.

You may find it easier to work with a partner.

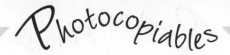

Exhibiting Clarice, see page 88

Boxes – Designing a design

You may have made the net of a cube in maths.

BUT

Could you make a box for your pencils?

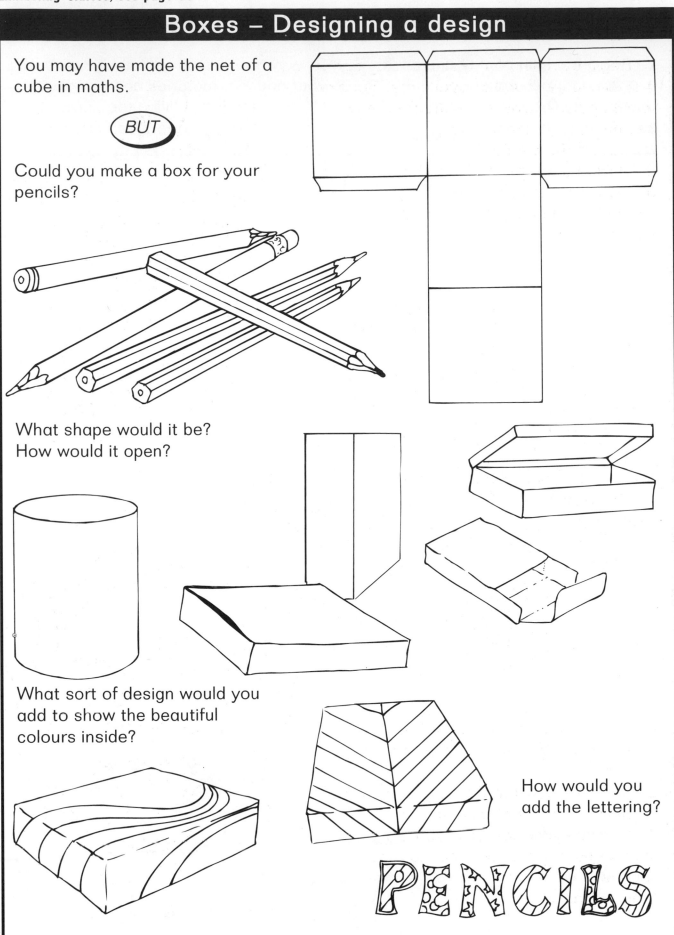

What shape would it be?
How would it open?

What sort of design would you add to show the beautiful colours inside?

How would you add the lettering?

PENCILS

Up against the wall, see page 91

Clay masks

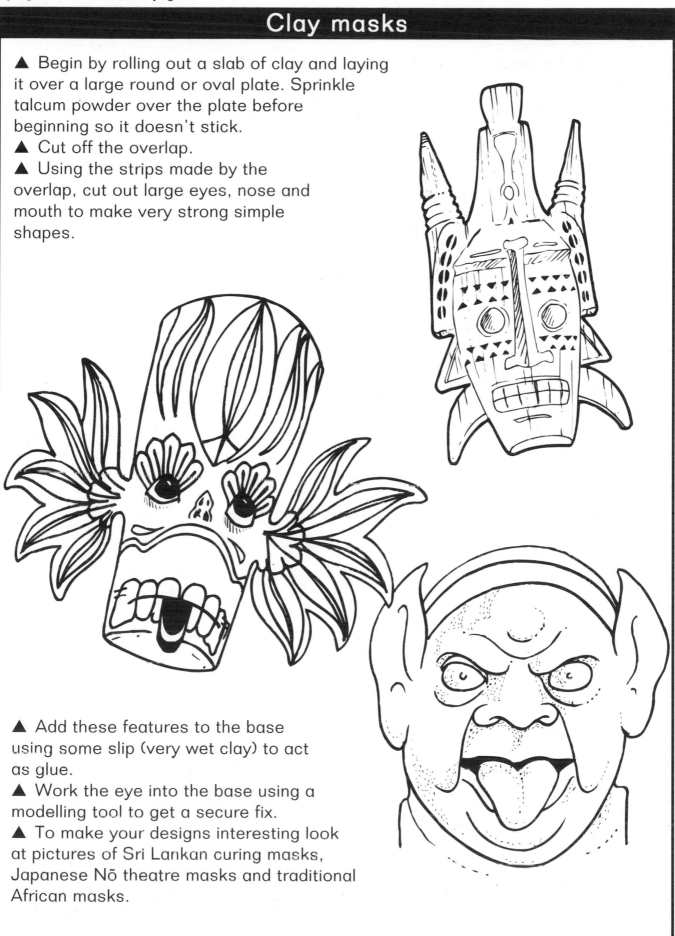

▲ Begin by rolling out a slab of clay and laying it over a large round or oval plate. Sprinkle talcum powder over the plate before beginning so it doesn't stick.
▲ Cut off the overlap.
▲ Using the strips made by the overlap, cut out large eyes, nose and mouth to make very strong simple shapes.

▲ Add these features to the base using some slip (very wet clay) to act as glue.
▲ Work the eye into the base using a modelling tool to get a secure fix.
▲ To make your designs interesting look at pictures of Sri Lankan curing masks, Japanese Nõ theatre masks and traditional African masks.

Bridge for all seasons, see page 93

A millennium tower

▲ Imagine your village, town or city asked you and your friend to design a tower for a special occasion, such as the new millennium celebrations!

▲ You have to build a model, not higher than 30cm tall, to show to the committee.

1 What will you make it out of?

2 Will you add symbols about life at the turn of the century...? OR will it just be bright and colourful and full of interesting shapes?

3 Will you draw your designs first... and then start to make your model?

4 Will it be solid or will you be able to see through it?

5 Will you paint pictures on it?

What will your tower look like?

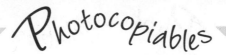

Mapping out a design, see page 98

How to find me

▲ Suppose I visited your school next week and needed to find you! Could you draw me a really interesting map, WITH NO WORDS, to show how I get from the school gates to you and your table?   *Remember NO WORDS!*

Gymnastic shapes, see page 100

Figurative shapes

Gymnasts make wonderful shapes.

▲ Can you draw five people...

...and then join the two ends together?

How would you paint your picture to make the design REALLY colourful?

▲ Try cutting the people out and rearranging them on another sheet of paper.

Circular sections, see page 102

A time design

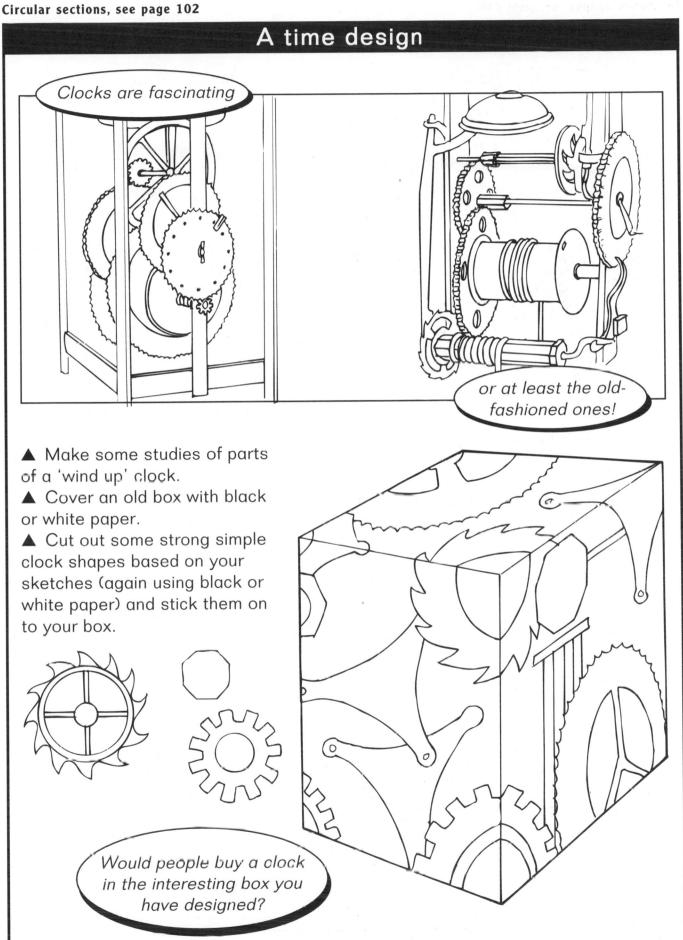

Clocks are fascinating

or at least the old-fashioned ones!

▲ Make some studies of parts of a 'wind up' clock.
▲ Cover an old box with black or white paper.
▲ Cut out some strong simple clock shapes based on your sketches (again using black or white paper) and stick them on to your box.

Would people buy a clock in the interesting box you have designed?

ART

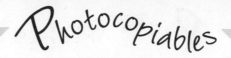

Jewels of the sea, see page 104

Reflections of the sea

If you were to make jewellery based on the theme of the 'sea', then you would need a mirror in which to admire your efforts.

Mirrors look best in frames whatever the shape...

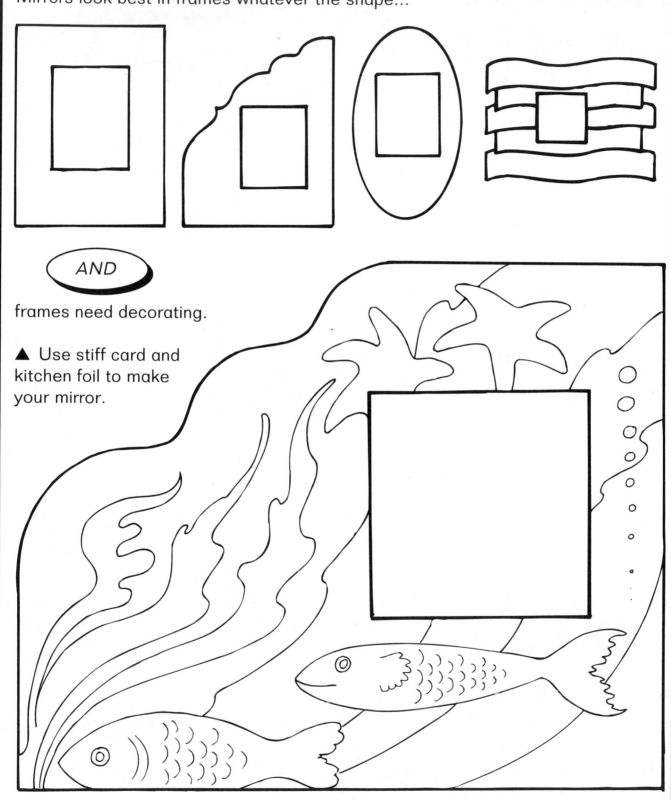

AND

frames need decorating.

▲ Use stiff card and kitchen foil to make your mirror.

ART

Improvising from music, see page 106

A picture fit for playing

▲ Imagine painting a picture for a musician to play!
Which musical instrument would be needed to play this drawing?

or this?

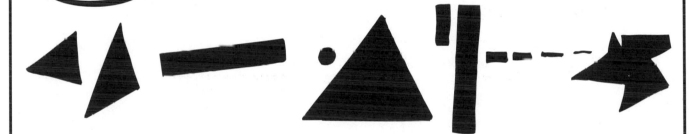

or even this?

▲ Can you design a picture using shapes, lines and colour for a musician to interpret? Practise some ideas to start with.

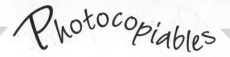

Enquiring into design, see page 27

Bizarre napkins

▲ Look very carefully at the floral design on the crockery in the middle of the poster. You have been commissioned by a company to design a matching napkin. What would your design look like?

Will you have a wide border with flowers in the middle?

OR

a narrow border? with lots of flowers?

OR

two borders? with flowers in between?

OR

Can you think of a more interesting arrangement?

Will you use different colours?

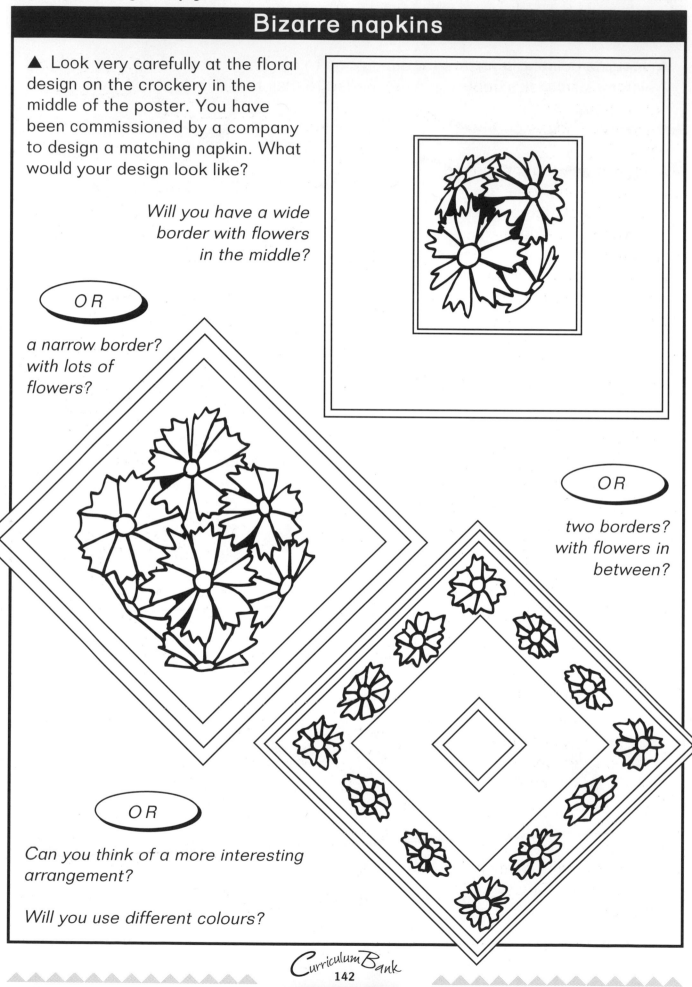

Enquiring into design, see page 27

Classy teapots

Teapots come in all shapes and sizes. There are three very unusual and distinctive shapes on this poster.

▲ How many teapots have you got in your home? Take some sketch paper home and make careful drawings.

▲ Now design your own teapot, but work to a theme.

Remember your teapot must be *functional* (in other words it must be able to pour).

You may combine all your teapots to make a small class book of 'Classy Teapots'.

Enquiring into design, see page 27

Clarice Cliff and Bizarre pottery

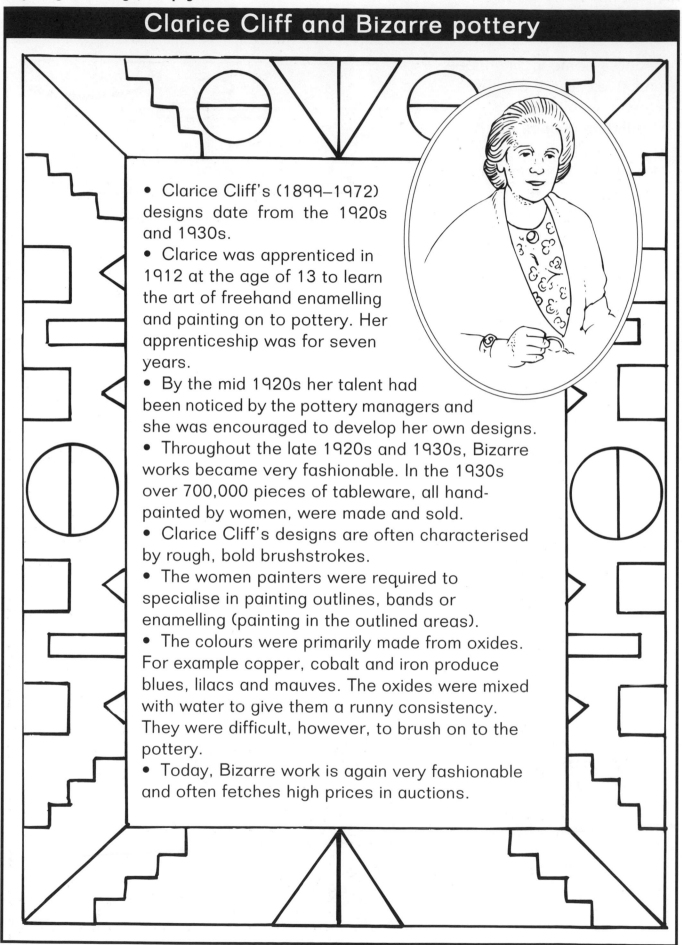

• Clarice Cliff's (1899–1972) designs date from the 1920s and 1930s.

• Clarice was apprenticed in 1912 at the age of 13 to learn the art of freehand enamelling and painting on to pottery. Her apprenticeship was for seven years.

• By the mid 1920s her talent had been noticed by the pottery managers and she was encouraged to develop her own designs.

• Throughout the late 1920s and 1930s, Bizarre works became very fashionable. In the 1930s over 700,000 pieces of tableware, all hand-painted by women, were made and sold.

• Clarice Cliff's designs are often characterised by rough, bold brushstrokes.

• The women painters were required to specialise in painting outlines, bands or enamelling (painting in the outlined areas).

• The colours were primarily made from oxides. For example copper, cobalt and iron produce blues, lilacs and mauves. The oxides were mixed with water to give them a runny consistency. They were difficult, however, to brush on to the pottery.

• Today, Bizarre work is again very fashionable and often fetches high prices in auctions.

Bizarre

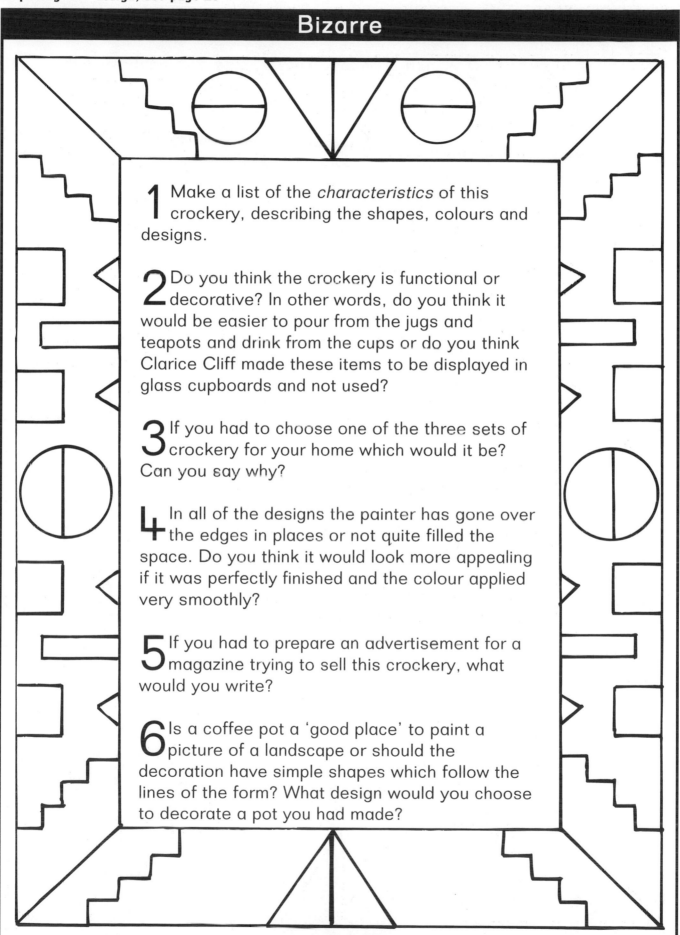

1 Make a list of the *characteristics* of this crockery, describing the shapes, colours and designs.

2 Do you think the crockery is functional or decorative? In other words, do you think it would be easier to pour from the jugs and teapots and drink from the cups or do you think Clarice Cliff made these items to be displayed in glass cupboards and not used?

3 If you had to choose one of the three sets of crockery for your home which would it be? Can you say why?

4 In all of the designs the painter has gone over the edges in places or not quite filled the space. Do you think it would look more appealing if it was perfectly finished and the colour applied very smoothly?

5 If you had to prepare an advertisement for a magazine trying to sell this crockery, what would you write?

6 Is a coffee pot a 'good place' to paint a picture of a landscape or should the decoration have simple shapes which follow the lines of the form? What design would you choose to decorate a pot you had made?

ART

Starting from Lowry, see page 43

When the sun came out to play!

Lowry's pictures often look as though they were painted on a cold day with snow threatening.

▲ Imagine that it is August, not November, and it's a beautiful warm summer's day. The shadows are short, the grass green and some people are even sunbathing!

Use lots of bright reds, yellows and blues to paint your picture.

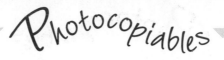

The games children play

A very famous Flemish painter, Pieter Bruegel, painted a picture called *Children's Games* way back in the sixteenth century. Is this picture in your school library? You will see that games with hoops and balls have been played by children for hundreds of years.

If you painted a picture of 'children's games' what games would you include? What games do you play in your school playground?

▲ Draw and paint a picture of children playing in your school playground.

ART

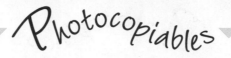

*P*hotocopiables

Starting from Lowry, see page 43

L S Lowry (1887–1976)

- Lowry is one of the most famous British 'northern' artists of the twentieth century.
- He was born in Manchester, studied at Manchester School of Art and relied on images of life in and around Manchester and Salford as the inspiration of much of his work.
- His paintings are instantly recognisable with their sombre colours, industrial backdrops, and 'antlike' or matchstick people, inhabiting an almost silent world.
- Despite his popularity he is not regarded as being an influential figure in twentieth-century British Art. Rather he fulfils the role model many people have of an artist; reclusive, independent and unworldly.
- His art is often considered as naive or primitive, as if painted by an untutored amateur. This is not true, for like almost all artists, Lowry studied diligently, attended art schools intermittently for 25 years and worked tirelessly at his painting.
- The Salford Museum and Art Gallery has established a permanent display of his paintings.

ART

Starting from Lowry, see page 43

The Playground

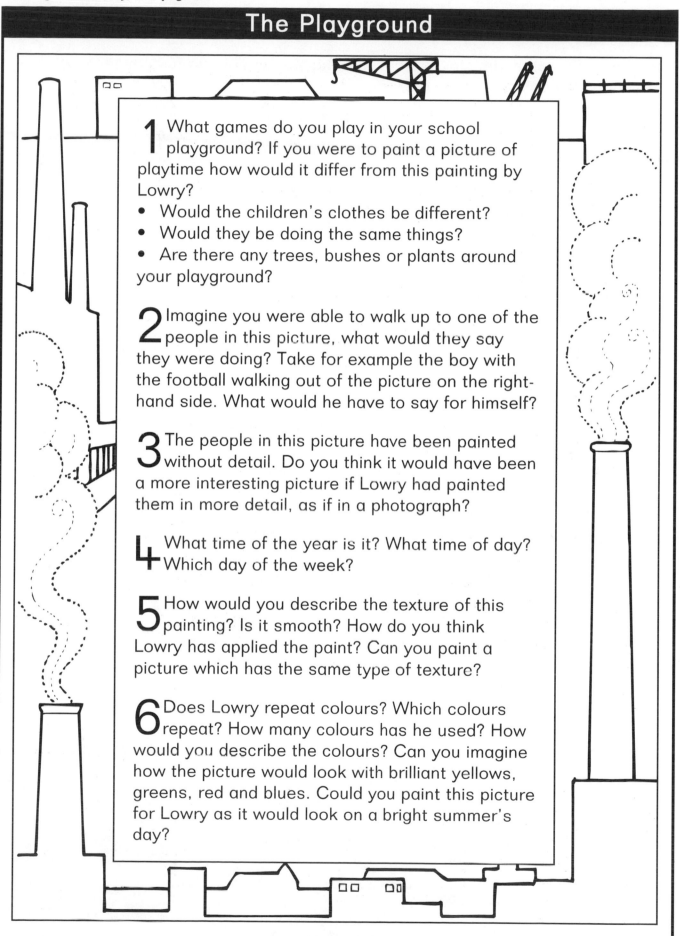

1 What games do you play in your school playground? If you were to paint a picture of playtime how would it differ from this painting by Lowry?
- Would the children's clothes be different?
- Would they be doing the same things?
- Are there any trees, bushes or plants around your playground?

2 Imagine you were able to walk up to one of the people in this picture, what would they say they were doing? Take for example the boy with the football walking out of the picture on the right-hand side. What would he have to say for himself?

3 The people in this picture have been painted without detail. Do you think it would have been a more interesting picture if Lowry had painted them in more detail, as if in a photograph?

4 What time of the year is it? What time of day? Which day of the week?

5 How would you describe the texture of this painting? Is it smooth? How do you think Lowry has applied the paint? Can you paint a picture which has the same type of texture?

6 Does Lowry repeat colours? Which colours repeat? How many colours has he used? How would you describe the colours? Can you imagine how the picture would look with brilliant yellows, greens, red and blues. Could you paint this picture for Lowry as it would look on a bright summer's day?

ART

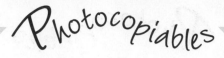

Fruit, jugs and Cézanne, see page 52

Printing still life

▲ Using the same items as Cézanne, make a series of careful outline drawings of apples, lemons, a plate and a jug.

▲ Use activity paper, thin card or textured wallpaper.

▲ Cut out your shapes and stick them on to stiff card.

▲ Make a very carefully organised arrangement for example:

like this   OR   like this

Think about shape and space as you work.

▲ Now roll printing ink across the surface and print your design.
If you are very careful you can print one colour after you have stuck on the plate and jug and a second one when the fruit has been added.

Remember to draw round the outline of the card so you can put in exactly the same place when you print the second colour.

Fruit, jugs and Cézanne, see page 52

Apple cards

▲ Look very, very carefully at the way in which Cézanne has painted the apples. Practise putting your paint on to paper working thickly so you can see each brushstroke.

▲ Can you find an apple to draw and paint? Work to exactly the size of the apple. Keep looking at your apple and at Cézanne's painting. Can you paint your apple in the same way?

REMEMBER
Keep mixing your colours to capture every change.

▲ When you have finished you might like to choose a card to mount your apple, which you can bend to form a greeting card. Against what colour card does your apple look most impressive?

Class 4's Apple Cards

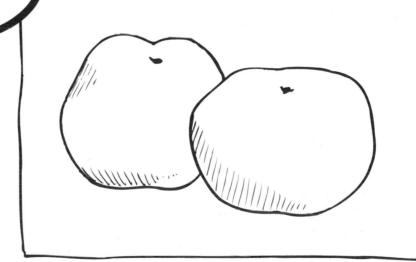

Fruit, jugs and Cézanne, see page 52

Paul Cézanne (1839–1906)

- We tend to refer to Cézanne as a 'Post-Impressionist'. In other words, his most well-known paintings date from the late 1880s and 1890s, just after the major Impressionist exhibitors. He was a contemporary of Van Gogh and Gauguin but not a close friend.
- While many of Cézanne's paintings include figures we primarily associate him with landscape and still life painting.
- When looking at Cézanne's still life paintings it is useful to get the children to look very carefully and in silence for some time. As they look, questions arise, for with Cézanne's work nothing is quite as it seems: tables are tilted, pieces of fruit look as if they are about to crash to the floor, and plates and bowls appear distorted.
- Remember that Cézanne is an artist, a painter, not a photographer. He is depicting apples, lemons, jugs and plates but he is also painting shapes and colours, using textures and making patterns. He is, therefore, an excellent artist to explore the 'elements of art', for example line, tone, shape, colour, pattern and texture.
- It is for these reasons that his work was so influential on many of the most important artists of the first half of the twentieth century including Picasso, Braque and Matisse.

Fruit, jugs and Cézanne, see page 52

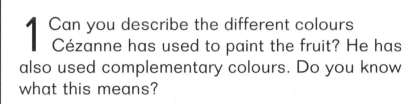

Still life/Cézanne

1 Can you describe the different colours Cézanne has used to paint the fruit? He has also used complementary colours. Do you know what this means?

2 How do you think Cézanne has applied the paint? Has he put on a thin colour wash, painted over some areas several times or used the paint thickly?

3 Look carefully at how Cézanne has arranged the fruit. Which fruit overlap and which are separate? Imagine this was a maze, how many ways can you get from the left-hand side of the table to the right? Could you arrange a still life where some objects overlapped and some were separate?

4 Can you think why Cézanne has not put the jug and the table in the middle of the picture so that it is symmetrical? If you make your picture symmetrical is it more interesting than when it appears more balanced to the left or right?

5 Do you think Cézanne was standing up and looking down on to the table or sitting looking across? Instead of putting an arrangement on a table, put it on the floor and draw the pattern you see. You may find your picture looks more interesting this way.

Rooftops and skylines, see page 68

Toledo – The complete story

If only El Greco had held his camera the other way up we would have been able to see more of the landscape and the rest of the town of Toledo.

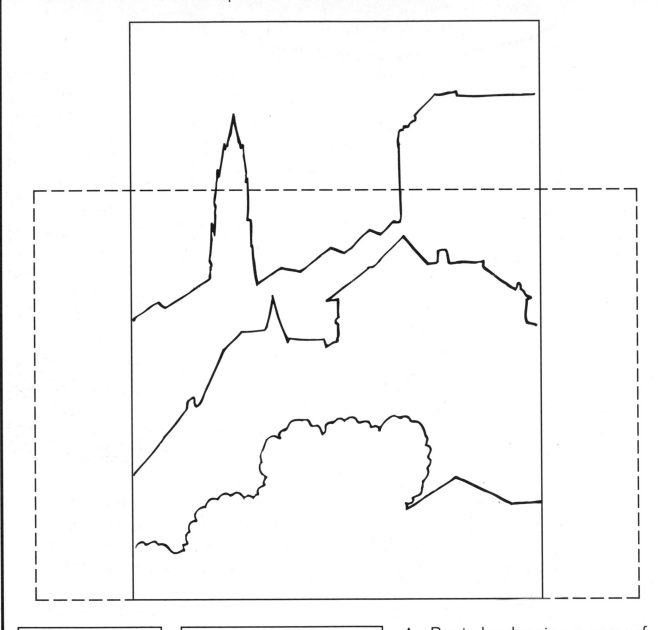

▲ Begin by drawing a copy of El Greco's picture of Toledo in the centre of a sheet of paper. Can you then add the landscape to the left and right?

Can you position your paper landscape and not portrait?

When you are pleased with your drawing you may wish to add colour.

ART

Rooftops and skylines, see page 68

Buildings in a landscape

When a builder wants to sell new houses on an estate he doesn't just show the houses.

He adds lots of trees and shrubs. Why?

Houses and buildings, and trees and shrubs make interesting pictures. From your classroom window can you see buildings among trees? Do you have a view of houses and trees from your bedroom window?

Can you produce a painting from a view you have observed of buildings and trees?

ART

Rooftops and skylines, see page 68

El Greco/Toledo (1541–1614)

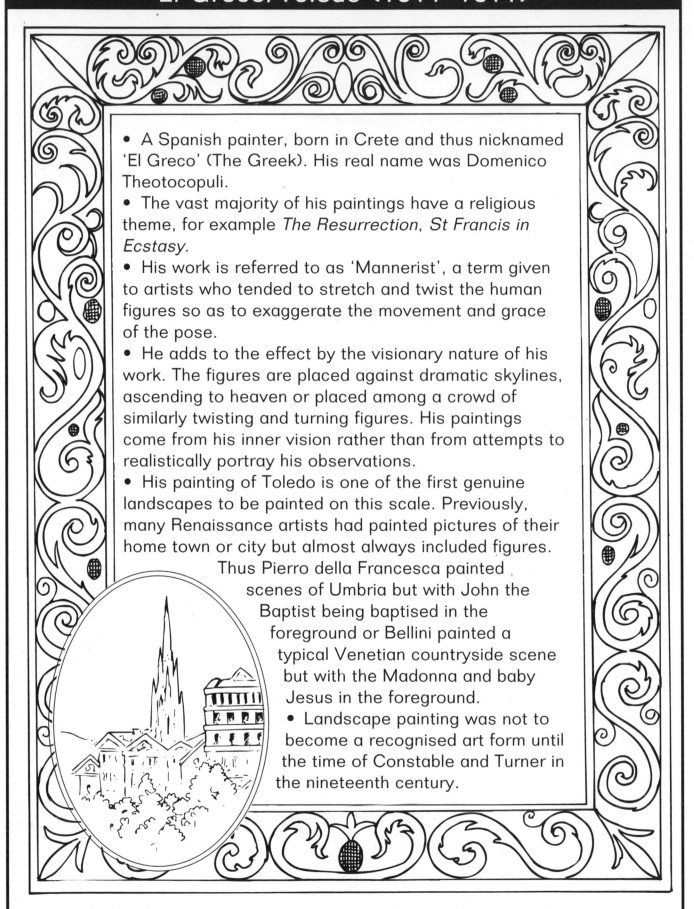

• A Spanish painter, born in Crete and thus nicknamed 'El Greco' (The Greek). His real name was Domenico Theotocopuli.

• The vast majority of his paintings have a religious theme, for example *The Resurrection*, *St Francis in Ecstasy*.

• His work is referred to as 'Mannerist', a term given to artists who tended to stretch and twist the human figures so as to exaggerate the movement and grace of the pose.

• He adds to the effect by the visionary nature of his work. The figures are placed against dramatic skylines, ascending to heaven or placed among a crowd of similarly twisting and turning figures. His paintings come from his inner vision rather than from attempts to realistically portray his observations.

• His painting of Toledo is one of the first genuine landscapes to be painted on this scale. Previously, many Renaissance artists had painted pictures of their home town or city but almost always included figures. Thus Pierro della Francesca painted scenes of Umbria but with John the Baptist being baptised in the foreground or Bellini painted a typical Venetian countryside scene but with the Madonna and baby Jesus in the foreground.

• Landscape painting was not to become a recognised art form until the time of Constable and Turner in the nineteenth century.

ART

Rooftops and skylines, see page 68

Toledo

1 Imagine you were standing next to El Greco as he silently painted this picture, what sounds would you hear?

2 As you look to left and right describe the view to both sides. Can you imagine how the whole view would look?

3 El Greco has not used brilliant blue and green. How would you describe the different blues and greens you can see?

4 Imagine you walked back to Toledo with El Greco once he had completed painting. Can you describe the walk? Would it be a difficult journey?

5 One famous writer described this picture by saying that it looks as though El Greco painted Toledo as if during an 'apocalyptic catastrophe'. Can you find out what this means? Do you agree with him?

6 Have you ever been outside and watched dark clouds rapidly move across the sky towards you? Could you paint a picture of an oncoming thunderstorm about to pass over your school, house or town? What colours would you use?

Storm over my school

INTEGRATING INFORMATION TECHNOLOGY WITHIN ART

Art is very much a practical subject and, although computers can enhance and extend children's experiences in this area, they should not replace the opportunity for practical hands-on exploration and experimentation with the full range of mark-making materials, tone, texture and colour. Indeed these experiences are essential if children are to make effective use of art and drawing software. It is also important for children to have a real purpose in using art software if they are to explore the full benefits of computer graphics.

The work of other artists provides a rich source of ideas, examples and creativity, and children can make use of information technology to find, store and use works of art. CD-ROMs contain many hundreds of pictures which can be displayed on screen or printed out. The Internet is now a rich source of both pictures and information about different artists. Both can be used to develop children's artistic skills.

Drawing and art packages

There is a vast array of art software available for children of all ages and it is important to ensure that as children's artistic skills develop, they are given opportunities to use more sophisticated software. A restrictive range of options, for example only having 16 colours to choose from, can limit the children.

Throughout this book two distinct types of software have been identified: art and drawing. Although they can achieve similar results they have distinct differences which makes them more suitable for particular activities.

Drawing software – Drawing packages enable children to draw lines and shapes and add text. The lines and shapes can be manipulated, resized, moved, stretched and rotated. A range of colours can be selected and used to fill shapes. On more sophisticated packages, the shapes can be combined to form a single 'object', so, for example, all the components of a flower can be drawn separately, combined and then kept as a flower. Text can be added and fonts, sizes and colours changed. In such packages it is easy to move shapes around the screen and position components of a picture wherever you wish. In order to help children line up the shapes and lines as they draw them, it is usually possible to have a background grid. When the 'snap to grid' option is turned, on the ends of the drawn lines are automatically connected to the nearest point on the background grid. This option makes it easy to line up shapes in a pattern.

Art and painting software – Art or painting packages use a different approach to drawing software. The drawing process is more akin to using a pencil or brush. Lines and shapes are drawn by colouring in the individual pixels of the screen. Very detailed work and effects can be produced to create pictures which, with skill, can mirror the results of paint on paper. Such packages usually have a range of tools, such as brushes, sprays and rollers, for adding and creating different effects. Text can be added, coloured and resized. These packages are often referred to as painting packages. The saved pictures can take up very large amounts of memory. Pictures taken from a CD-ROM or from the Internet will be in a format that enables them to be viewed from within an art package.

The skills that children need to be taught using such software are similar to word processing, but related to pictures. They will need to know how to:
- select appropriate tools for line drawing (to draw thin and detailed lines); drawing straight and curved lines using freehand tools; brushes (to draw thicker lines); sprays (to spray colours or create a different line effect); rollers (to fill in areas of colour);
- change features of different tools to affect the thickness of lines; the size and shape of brushes; the density of sprays;
- draw different lines and shapes including squares; rectangles; circles and ellipses;
- edit and erase shapes and lines to duplicate shapes or use a 'stamp' facility;
- use the undo facility to erase the last action;
- resize, rotate and move shapes and lines;
- select parts of a drawing and join them together;
- use the undo facility to erase the last action;
- resize and rotate shapes and lines;
- move and flip shapes and lines around the screen;
- fill shapes with colours;
- select colours from a simple or complex palette;
- 'mix' their own colours and patterns;
- add, resize and colour text;
- zoom into parts of the picture for detailed work;
- clear the screen or start again;
- save and retrieve their work from a disk;
- set up the printer and print out their work.

Using pictures from other sources

In this book the work of other artists is used to highlight particular techniques or approaches. High quality pictures are now available from many CD-ROMs and can be downloaded from the Internet.

Suitable pictures can be found on many CD-ROMs. Some, such as *Art in the National Curriculum* are compilations specially prepared for the National Curriculum, while others, such as *Microsoft's Art Gallery* are simply a large collection of pictures. The pictures can usually be saved from the CD-ROM on to the hard disk and then loaded into a suitable viewer or art package. They can then be printed out or viewed on screen. The final quality will not be as good as a photograph or print, but will provide a useful resource. Children can also 'browse' the collection to see a wider range of pictures from a particular artist.